FATHER'S ROOM

By

Helen Resneck-Sannes

ISBN: 1-4033-8942-X (e-book)
ISBN: 1-4033-8943-8 (Paperback)

Library of Congress Control Number: 2002095436

This book is printed on acid free paper.

Printed in the United States of America
Bloomington, IN

1stBooks – rev. 11/27/02

"Families name us and define us, give us strength, give us grief. All our lives we struggle to embrace or escape their influence. They are magnets that both hold us close and drive us away."
(George Howe Colt, P.48 "The Sun", June 1999, Issue 282)

"The words a father speaks to his children in the privacy of the home are not overheard at the time, but, as in whispering galleries, they will be clearly heard at the end and by posterity."
(Jean-Paul Richter, p.48)

Dedication

This book is dedicated to the psychiatrists, doctors, lawyers, nursing home attendants, wives, husbands, daughters, sons, and grandchildren - - to all those people who care about and care for our old people suffering from dementia.

Acknowledgments

I am grateful to Vito Victor, Carol Whitehill, and Deborah Turner for reading numerous versions of this book and providing encouragement and guidance. I also wish to thank Patrice Vecchione for assisting me with finding the authentic voice and for great bike rides up and down the hills of Santa Cruz. And a special thank you to Ellen Bass for her editing of the book. She not only has been a good friend for 25 years, but has also supported the writer in me.

I want to thank my brothers for their love, humor, and for providing the material for this book.

Finally, a thank you to David, my husband. On our second date he came to the door with his lips glued shut, on our third date he encouraged me to jump off a cliff while he held the lines, and has never turned away from the adventures and challenges of our life together.

PART 1
MARION, INDIANA

The rains have been heavy this year. It's June in Marion, Indiana, my home town, and I drive with the windows rolled down, inhaling the smell of damp earth and new grass. I have come for Dad and plan to bring him back to California, to Santa Cruz, where I live.

As I turn into Shady Hills, I'm once again struck by the expanse of land each house commands. I follow the winding tree lined lane past houses set back from the road on hills, so that each home appears to be surrounded by its own park. When Myrrhia, my daughter was a baby, she ran on the grass in front of the houses. I told her to come back that was someone else's land. "All of this belongs to one family?" she voiced with three-year-old astonishment. I turn left off the major drive and at the end of the lane, sits our house, well really my dad's house.

I park the car in front, but can't remove the key from the ignition in the rental car. It's stuck in one of those special locking devices. Dad opens the front door and comes out. He's a tall man, 6 feet 2 inches and wears size thirteen shoes. He was the oldest son, went to Harvard on a scholarship and always takes charge. He still has his hair, although gray and thin. He approaches the car with his characteristic long-legged stride, his shoulders back and head held high. When younger, I had to run to keep up with him.

He smiles and I'm happy to see that he has replaced the front tooth that was missing last summer and has resumed his stately handsome appearance. "Hi Helen. You're here. I didn't know when you were coming."

I had sent him a letter in addition to our phone calls, so that he would have a record of when I arrived, but he forgot anyway. "Hi Dad. Yes, I'm here."

"Why don't you turn off the car engine?"

"I can't get the key out of the lock."

"Maybe I can help." He reaches in the window over me, finds a button that I hadn't noticed before, twists and turns the key and pulls it out. "There. Where's your bag?"

"In the trunk."

Although his cheeks are pink, he is quite thin. I wonder if he has been eating since Dorothy, his wife, left. He easily lifts the bag and heads up the walk. I'm anxious about being alone with him, and Dusty, my younger brother doesn't arrive until tomorrow. The next door neighbor sent me e-

1

mail that Dad kicked him when he came to retrieve the round dining room table Dorothy had sold him. Dad had papers on that table and didn't want him to take it. The neighbor pushed his way into the house anyway. Dad kicked him and then called the police. They told the neighbor that he couldn't force his way into a house, and Dad was temporarily mollified. Although aggressive and competitive, my dad had never been violent and the behavior surprised and frightened me.

When I described my dad's behavior to a colleague, he told me about his father who also had Alzheimers. His dad had become verbally aggressive and his mother was frightened that he might hurt her physically so she called the police. When they came, he hit one of the policemen with a telephone. They placed his dad in the psychiatric ward, and he died that night from a medication overdose given by the psychiatrists. Not only am I concerned about my father's the state of mind, I'm also worried about the condition of the house. My dad hasn't been able to file his taxes in three years, and the house is filling with papers. Dorothy has been gone for two months and I'm afraid nothing's been thrown away or cleaned since then.

But when I follow him into the house, I'm surprised that it doesn't look too bad, only stacked with papers, which I expected. He seems like the warm energetic competent father I have always known, and I think that maybe he will be all right and that he can stay in his home after all. I begin to walk from the living room to the kitchen for a glass of water when he launches into a virulent tirade. At first I can't make out the words. All I notice is the anger in his voice. As the meaning becomes foreground against the background of rage, my hopes are immediately shattered. "You won't believe this. Everyone thinks that he's such a nice guy but he's come into the house, stolen my papers and broken into my car."

I stop walking and turn toward him, "are you certain you haven't misplaced them?" As Billy, my older brother used to say even when my dad was young, "I'm afraid if I put my hand on Dad's desk that I'll never be able to find it again."

"He's taken them," my dad insists.

"Why would he want to do that?" I ask.

"Nobody believes me, but I know that he wants my things." Dad's voice is loud and angry. He raises his fist. "I'm getting even with him. I'm breaking into his car tomorrow while he's at the Kiwanis meeting."

I'm worried but decide to change the subject. Hopefully he will forget about this by tomorrow.

The next morning he hasn't forgotten. In fact, now he has a plan for finding a locksmith and having a key altered to fit the neighbor's car. I remind him that we need to leave for Indianapolis soon. We plan to pick up Dusty at the airport and then go to the psychiatrist's office.

He yells that we have enough time and leaves to find the locksmith. I go into the kitchen and fix myself a piece of toast and a cup of instant coffee. I could search through the 20 different white cabinets for a coffee maker and some decent ground coffee or decaf, but I know from years of visits that this is a virgin kitchen that has never been defiled by gourmet roasted beans. At least Dorothy left some instant coffee.

The Marion Chronicle is a small paper; not much happens here. In about fifteen minutes I have finished reading it from cover to cover when I hear Dad's car pull into the garage. I put down the coffee and meet him at the top of the basement stairs. He looks downcast and discouraged. "I went to the Kiwanis meeting and that thief's car wasn't there," he says. "Nobody was there."

"When does the Kiwanis meet?" I ask him.

"It has met at the same time and day for years," he replies angrily. "But today they changed it."

"But what day does it meet?" I ask him.

"I don't remember these things."

"Well, today is Thursday."

We look at his calendar and Kiwanis meets on Wednesday. Alzheimers is such a strange disease, but it sometimes has its safety nets.

Dad's difficulties were brought to the attention of my brothers and me about a year ago. Dorothy, Dad's second wife had been calling us with reports of his unusual behavior. My mother died in November of 1981 from acute leukemia. He took excellent care of her throughout her illness. After working a full day, he would drive an hour and a half from Marion to Indianapolis to visit her in the hospital. Sometimes, he spent the night on the floor of her room.

Maybe the Alzheimers had begun invading his brain then. While my mother was dying, he began having difficulty throwing things away. When my two brothers Bill and Dusty, and I went home for her funeral, Dad said we all had to clear our own plates and load the dishwasher. I walked into the kitchen to find my older brother Billy holding his plate. His head was bent down and all I could see were his dark loose curls. His glasses were lying on the counter and his shoulders were shaking. Of course, Mom had just died and he and I were falling into crying episodes quite regularly.

"What's wrong?" I asked.

He put down his plate and wiped the tears from his eyes. After he'd arranged his glasses on his nose, he spoke with unusual slowness. "I've set up the recycling center for the city of Berkeley family camp, the Grand

Canyon and Tuolomne River trips, but I can't figure out how to throw anything away in my own kitchen."

I looked at the five different containers. I thought that the large white kitchen waste basket was probably for paper, the brown paper bag for cans, the bucket for plastics and the blue plastic pail for compost. Marion, Indiana didn't have a recycling center, so it wasn't clear why he had so many containers.

"I think you've figured out Dad's system."

"No garbage is supposed to leave this house?" he asked.

Dad walked in. "What are you doing?"

"I can't throw anything away," answered Billy

"Here. Let me have your plate." Dad stood in front of his five different receptacles, looked at each of them, put the plate down and left the kitchen. Billy and I cleaned up the best we could.

My brothers and I took turns staying with Dad. During each visit I closely inspected the house for changes. My bedroom had the same twin beds and electric blue satin bedspreads that were so popular in the sixties. The furniture in the living room and pictures on the walls were never changed. Dad hadn't numbered the twenty cabinets in the kitchen, as he had always threatened, although it never seemed such a bad idea. After Mom's death all the rooms remained the same except for my brother's. Lying on each bed was newspaper with decaying oranges, lemons, and other biodegradable items. I called each of my siblings to let them know that he was using their old bedroom as a compost pile. None of us ever thought that this might be the beginning stages of his Alzheimers.

Dad wants to drive to Indianapolis. As it may be one of the last times he is legally able to drive, I agree. This is a generous gesture on my part. He never has been a cautious driver. Two summers ago he took the off ramp from the highway at 70 miles per hour and then slammed on the brakes as we entered the main road. I had a headache the rest of that day.

The irony is that he taught me how to drive. We practiced parallel parking by sighting the angle to turn the car between two trees, which were stand ins for other vehicles. The first couple of times, I had difficulty lining up the car and either the front or back end was sticking out a little too far. Dad continually told me to sight on a line. I told him that I was sighting correctly but the trees were moving. It's odd to be the one in charge of whether he can drive.

Instead of staying on the interstate, he picks a circuitous route requiring numerous turns down various country roads and tree lined lanes bordered by gracious homes. Several times he forgets and turns the wrong direction and has to double back to find his way. However, given the complexity of the route he has chosen, his memory doesn't seem to be all that bad. I don't know if I could remember such a maze.

Driving to Indianapolis and picking up Dusty is no problem, but finding the neurological building at Indiana University Medical Center-- Alzheimers or no Alzheimers-- is a challenge. We wander around to different buildings asking questions, following directions only to find that we have arrived at the chemistry building or the emergency ward. Although my father has been there before, he isn't able to offer much help. We walk at least three miles trying to find the place. A green bench under a large oak tree beckons me to sit awhile and close my eyes, but I'm afraid that we will be late and miss the appointment. Luckily Dad isn't physically disabled. In fact, he seems to have more energy than Dusty and I together and I am a triathlete, at least I thought I was. I'm beginning to wonder if Dad isn't manic.

We finally drag ourselves into the testing center. I announce our names to the receptionist and tell her: "We had a difficult time finding you."

She responds coldly: "Oh."

More people come in--some red-faced, others pale, drenched in sweat and looking faint. They all talk about how difficult it is to find the center. The receptionist maintains her stance and says: "Oh," to each one of them.

Dr. Hendrie comes out and introduces himself to Dusty and me. We have exchanged letters about Dad and spoken on the phone once. I am pleased to find that the image I'd conjured of him and his actual self are similar. He is medium height, with thinning hair and a face that is warm and pleasant. He offers his hand and his manner, although friendly, is businesslike. He explains that he is having Dad tested in a separate room and will come back and talk with us.

Dusty and I try to read magazines, but I can't concentrate. In a quiet voice; I don't want the others in the room to hear that my dad was attempting to commit an illegal act; I begin telling Dusty about Dad trying to break into the neighbor's car when

Dr. Hendrie appears again. "While your father is finishing up his test, I thought we could take this opportunity to talk." He escorts Dusty and me into a room with a long table and fluorescent lights. It reminds me of the classrooms in the psychology building at the University of Wisconsin where I was a graduate student. No hint of fabric or color appears to soften the room. I guess all psychiatry and psychology departments ignore exterior space. Dr. Hendrie begins by saying: "Your father tests in the average range intellectually for a man his age."

"Does that mean he doesn't have Alzheimers?" Dusty asks.

But Dad has never been average, I think to myself. He always has been a little quirky.

5

Dr. Hendrie continues. "This is the third time I've tested him. He showed signs of incipient Alzheimers last year but there is a marked change this time with much more deterioration. We have to remember his starting IQ base and this is quite a loss. I interviewed him and his judgment and reasoning show marked shifts. I understand that his wife has left him. Is there anyone to help?"

"I'm prepared to take him back with me. We're meeting with his lawyer tomorrow. Hopefully, he will sign a power of attorney. I also wanted to talk to you about medication for him. My husband is a family practice physician and has placed Dad on Effexor, thinking he might be depressed."

"That is not a good drug for him. It's probably contributing to his problem." Dr. Hendrie is adamant. "Don't you know that physicians shouldn't treat members of their own family?"

Of course I'm aware of that, but David only wanted to help. It's so easy to rely on him and Dad has always trusted and respected him more than other doctors. I'm a psychologist and when I was first alerted to Dad's cognitive decline, I read a couple of neuropsychology texts and went to several conferences on Alzheimers. I learned that some of the patients benefited from antidepressants. Obviously, this is not the case with Dad, so I decide not to bring it up. Instead I ask Dr. Hendrie, "what would you suggest that Dad be taking?"

"Risperdal. I think that would be good for him. He should see a psychiatrist in Santa Cruz as soon as possible. What do you say we bring him in now."

Dr. Hendrie begins. "Mr. Resneck, it appears there has been quite a loss from the last time I tested you. As you know, when you were tested last May, we discussed the probability of this happening. You have Alzheimers and need to make accommodations. Someone should be handling your affairs and I don't think you should be driving or living alone anymore."

Dad's face tightens. "What do you mean? Just because of that little test, my life has to end? I can count backwards by threes, see 100, 97, 92, 91. No, that's not it. Let me try again, 95, 92, 81. It's a trick test anyway. Can you count backwards by threes, Helen? Let me see you do it."

I ignore his question and answer, "I know this is upsetting. But we love you. It's time for another stage of life."

"What other stage of life?" The volume of his voice is beginning to rise. "I have things to do. I don't want another stage of life. There is nothing wrong with me."

Dr. Hendrie looks at Dusty and me and shakes his head. He turns his attention to Dad. "You're fighting your children and they love you. They came all this way to help you. Is this what you want to do?"

"I know they came to help me, but it's sometimes hard to be helped. I don't want to be helped. I don't know if I can get used to this."

Dorothy and Dad married about 5 years after Mom died and he seemed okay for awhile. I was instrumental in having Dorothy and Dad get together. Although they lived in Indianapolis, Mom and Dad had known Dorothy and her husband for several years. They shared friends in Indianapolis and entertained with the same people. At one such party, when I was in my senior year at the University of Wisconsin, my mother mentioned to Dorothy that my roommate had become pregnant and there was a bedroom available in the house. Dorothy's daughter, Carol was beginning graduate school there and the two mothers decided that it would be good if their daughters met and perhaps, lived together. Carol called me on the phone and I liked her well enough that I thought she might work out as a roommate. It was in the middle of the year and I didn't have any other prospects.

Carol is 5 feet two inches tall with thick dark hair, olive skin and large intelligent brown eyes. Although I am taller, thinner with lighter hair and complexion, men often confused us. Maybe it's because we both have large breasts and men never get past the level of our chests to check out our faces. To add to the confusion we both dated several Davids, and our third roommate was also named Carol. When a David called asking for a Carol, none of us knew how to respond. We thought maybe people should stop using names all together and give their social security number instead.

Carol and I became good friends. During graduate school, we supported each other through our doctoral exams by being available to play two handed bridge during study breaks. Her first job was teaching at UCLA and mine at Kaiser Permanente in Los Angeles. I didn't like Los Angeles and was able to secure a job on the Monterey Bay, where I had always longed to live. However, it was difficult leaving Carol, and I drove off sobbing, knowing that it was time to find a partner and begin a family, and that we would never live together again.

Almost ten years later I was visiting Carol in Los Angeles. My mother had been dead for a couple of years and her mother had been widowed for at least twice as long. We were sitting on the beach when Carol said to me shyly, "My mom wants to date your dad."

"Really." Well, I'll tell him."

"She says there are all these women after him." Carol and I had gone through several years of falling in and out of love with various men. These guys were intellectually interesting and physically desirable, but we could never arrive at the point in the relationship where we wanted to share a home and children with them. Or maybe it wasn't the men at all, and neither Carol nor I were available for that kind of commitment. Now, we were talking about our parents dating. I started to have images of Dorothy and my Dad having dinner and then kissing. As their lips started to meet, the frame froze and then exploded. I looked at Carol with wide disbelieving eyes. She and I rarely needed to talk in complete sentences as we already knew what the other was thinking. She nodded her head "yes" in understanding and then said out loud: "I know."

I responded with, "Enough said about that, but Carol, there is something else. Do you know what this means if they like each other?"

"We'll be sisters." We both laughed.

My mom and dad had a running joke whenever he came home late, my mom teased that he was with "another woman" who she called Dorothy. The reality, as far as I know, is that neither of my parents had affairs, not that my dad didn't like pretty, vivacious women. But it's funny how this innocent joke had a prescient knowing. Amazingly, when Dad did remarry it was to Carol's mother, Dorothy. They were happy with each other, and the house began to look like a home again. One time, when I was visiting, Dorothy asked me to come down to the basement with her to look at some things she had found while cleaning up. She handed me a valentine card my mom had given to Dad as she was dying. It said: "I know that I'm not much fun, but I love you and you love me. I'm dying and you need to go on and find your Dorothy." As I read the card, the cool damp of the basement seized hold of my spine. I looked at her for a reaction, but she just watched with me with soft eyes. "Do you know about their joke, you know, I mean Mom and Dad's teasing about Dorothy?"

"Yes, your dad explained it to me. Your mom really loved your dad. It's in this card."

Images of my mom and dad in the car, sitting at the dinner table, and on the couch together flashed in front of my eyes. Although I felt a deep gratitude to Dorothy for showing me the card, I began missing my mom. I felt uncomfortable discussing this with Dorothy, so I just thanked her for showing me the card.

After they had been together five years I began receiving frequent telephone calls from Dorothy regarding Dad. At first the manager at Wal-Mart was calling her saying that Dad was wandering around and couldn't find his way out. He had given the manager his phone number to call Dorothy. She told the manager to show Dad the exit and that he would take care of himself after that. I had never been in a Wal-Mart but Dad was developing a fascination with the store. People assured me that Wal-Mart was a big building and it was easy to get lost there. The largest building I could imagine was Macys, but I was quickly corrected that Wal-Mart was different. The entire cavernous store was on one level, about three times the size of a K-Mart and contained everything that was needed to sustain life-- food, water, bedding, clothes, and electronic supplies.

That summer, July 1995, I went to visit him and he did seem a little strange. He was missing one front tooth. It's funny how different a person can look just because of a small hole in the mouth. When he smiled, my mom and I had thought he looked like Jimmy Stewart, but the space in his mouth caused him to look more like Daffy Duck. The house had begun to fill with papers, so I offered to help him sort through some of them. He and I went down to the basement. On a table mounded with other letters and magazines was a Newsweek dated April, 1995. I picked it up and showed it to Dad. "This is dated April, do you still want to read it?"

"Let me see." He picked it up and looked at it, and put it down. "Yes, I think I need that."

A few minutes later I found some checks he hadn't cashed and bills he needed to pay. Once again, I picked up the Newsweek and showed it to him. Again he insisted that he wanted to keep it. Five minutes later he picked up the very same

Newsweek that we had already discussed two times and said: "When did this magazine arrive? It looks interesting."

"You don't remember us talking about it a minute ago?"

"No, I've never seen it before." I knew then that something was not okay.

In January, 1996 Dorothy called my brothers and me to tell us that she was thinking of leaving. Dad became furious if she tried to clean or move anything in the house. She warned us that she couldn't live with him any longer and that we, his children needed to take over. Finally, she delivered an ultimatum. She would stay with him until April and then was leaving. She said that she had offered to have him come live with her in her condominium in Indianapolis, but she wouldn't spend another winter in the country. The house was only a mile from the town of Marion, but he lived on county roads. Sometimes it was a day or two before the plows removed the snow. I also think Dorothy was tired of sharing Dad's house, where he wouldn't allow her to move anything or fix it the way she liked.

Although I didn't like the idea of my dad being abandoned, I understood her point of view. They'd had only a few good years together and now he was angry and unmanageable. She wanted out.

Even though Dad insisted he was fine, I received daily calls from people in Marion who respected him and were concerned. I started writing down the names and phone numbers of the callers and the incidents they were reporting. One night he was stopped in the park at 2:00 am by the police. He told them that he was on his way to a bagel brunch. He became lost on the way to a Bat Mitzvah in Tennessee and ended up spending a couple of nights in his car. He never made it to the celebration which as it turned out had occurred a month before. Another night he showed up at the emergency room of the hospital. He was afraid that he was not getting enough oxygen to his muscles. The mental health center sent a representative to the hospital to interview him, but no follow up or treatment plan was considered. It was ironic. Mom had been the president of the county mental health board and now Dad was being evaluated as a possible patient. He called two of his friends, Dick Simons and Grant Russell to take him home.

He voiced his opinions loudly, often screaming. People were breaking into his house and stealing his things. He insisted he was fine, although another part of himself knew he wasn't.

Bill, the eldest, and a lawyer asked Dad to sign over a power of attorney, giving him control of his assets.   Dad was intellectually deteriorating and needed someone to help manage his affairs, but he refused. I wrote several letters, in which I tried to convince Dad that he needed help, urging him to give Bill the power of attorney, but Dad was adamant in his refusal to trust Billy.

Dusty and I concocted all sorts of plans to rescue Dad. Dusty offered to drive him across country to California; but lucky for him, Dad refused. I looked for a bigger house so there would be space for Dad to live with us. Bill wisely tried to discourage us from these plans.

"Dad is crazy," he told me. Without a power of attorney, you will have to pay for everything. He's too paranoid to trust anyone."

"But we have to do something," I insisted. "What will happen to him?"

"Leave him naked screaming in the streets. Then he'll be taken care of by the law."

"Are you serious?   Could you allow your father to run through the streets naked?"

"Look," he replied in a calmer voice. "He won't sign a power of attorney, he's paranoid about money, so you'll have to pay for any care facility or plane flight out of your own money. You don't know how crazy he is. Without a power of attorney, you'll just have to let him do what he is going to do."

Dusty and I couldn't tolerate that thought. I was worried and scared. I tried to maintain constant phone contact while I worked with his lawyer to set up a power of attorney. Although Dad wouldn't trust his oldest son to handle his affairs; maybe he would trust me.

During this time my and husband, David and I spent a week river rafting the Grand Canyon. We had decided to only raft the first part of the river and hiked out from the bottom of the canyon. I hadn't been able to speak to Dad for five days, so on reaching the lodge at the top, my first act was to call him from a pay phone. I waited anxiously, staring at the phone while it rang. I heard a voice that said; "This is Bill Resneck. When you hear the beep, now here's the beep..." He then yelled: "Hang up. Hang up." Of course I obeyed my father and hung up.

That didn't work, I said to myself. I called again and left the phone number of the lodge where David and I were staying on the answering machine. Then I went to find David in the gift shop. "How's your Dad?"

"He has this strange message on the answering machine which tells you to hang up without time for leaving a message."

"Sounds interesting. Do you like this hat? Look it's soft and will keep us warm at night in the tent."

I realized that we were both tired from the hike; and besides, I didn't feel like discussing Dad right now. "Sure, I want it in green. How about you get that black one?"

Later that night when Dad returned my call and reassured me that he was okay, I asked him about the message.

"Oh, I have that message to save money. If you hang up then you don't have to pay for the long distance call." He had other great ideas... like it's always better to enter the exit because there aren't any cars ahead of you.

So, now it's June and Dusty drives the car back from the Indiana University Medical Center to Marion, choosing a direct route. That night we go to dinner at Dad's favorite restaurant which is a steak house with a huge salad bar. Dad wants to drive. I think to myself, "why not?" He may never drive again. We enter the door and sitting at the first booth is Margaret, a woman who worked for Dad at his store for 20 years. She has the same gray curly hair and round smiling face. Dad walks by without recognizing her. I give her a hug.

"Why, Helen Rae," she says. Many of the people in Marion still include my middle name which was my grandmother's. "What a pleasure to see you. How are you doing?"

"It's not easy right now. Dusty and I have come to take care of Dad. He's agreed to come back with me to California. The psychiatrist told us he shouldn't drive."

"I know your Dad isn't doing well. We all see what a hard time he's having. You're doing the right thing."

I was grateful for her understanding.

"My mother became forgetful," she continued, "I was afraid she would leave the stove on and burn the place down. I moved her out of her house and into mine. I took care of her for 10 years and she was so angry with me that she wouldn't say my name. For 10 years my mother would never call me by my name. Your father loves you," she adds. "I'll never forget that summer you insisted on hitch hiking through Europe alone. He was upset all summer."

"Really? But he never said anything. Mom tried to talk me out of it for months, but Dad said he was supporting my independence."

"Well, he never said anything to you, but believe me, he was worried."

I couldn't understand why he would put himself through that kind of worry. I had saved $1,000 from babysitting and waitressing, and I didn't want to spend money on the train. I told them I would use a pass if they bought it; and even though Mom had wanted to purchase a Eurail pass for me, Dad objected on the grounds that he didn't want to interfere with my trip. I made it through that summer. If my young daughter, decides to go to Europe for the summer, I'm buying her the pass.

That night Dad is upset. "Why can't I drive?" he screams in my face.

I look at him and with calm words, which don't match at all how I feel on the inside, I reply. "Because you aren't the only one that matters. We care about you and worry. The police have had to stop and take care of you. What if you injured someone in your car? You have had wonderful years of managing your life. You've done a fine job as head of the family and supported us all. Now, you are entering a different time of life. It's our turn to help you."

He is quiet and looks at me. My eyes burn and I feel a tear slide down my cheek. "I love you. This is hard for all of us. I know how difficult it is for you."

The next morning I pull Dusty aside. He is the youngest but the biggest of the three children. At an even six feet, he towers over me. Although he is not as tall as Dad, who's 6 foot two, Dusty's bones are fuller, which make him seem larger. His eyes are the same blue green as Mom's. Dad referred to her eyes as "limpid pools of water". I always had a hard time with that expression. As a child, I thought about the dog limping and wondered if Mom's eyes weren't damaged in some way.

Dusty's straight, sandy, blond hair became dark and curly at puberty and is now turning gray and receding from his forehead. Unlike Bill and I, who finished college and became professionals, Dusty left school during his sophomore year and has his own landscape business. My father still holds out his verdict on whether Dusty is a success or not.

I appreciate him coming to Marion with me and value his opinion. I look up at his concerned face and ask: "Do you think we should go to the lawyer's office? Dad is upset. I'm afraid this will stir him up more."

"We've come this far. Let's keep going. I'll be there too."

I want to hug him but only respond with a quiet, "Thank you."

Dad introduces Dusty and me to his lawyer, Mr. Holderead, who he calls, "Jerry". I've already spoken to him on the phone and am pleased to put a friendly face with the voice. He is a short man with balding hair, a warm smile and a firm handshake. I can see that Dad likes him. Still, my legs are shaking as we enter the conference room. We sit down at a massive dark table made of mahogany. The curtains are heavy wine brocade and the carpet is a thick rich brown. The chairs are large and solid. The ambience suggests old money.

Dad takes a piece of paper out of his pocket. "I have some business I need taken care of. I think I spoke to you about this on the phone. Let's begin with the furnace and heating company. Those people over-charged me. I have the bill." He start rummaging through his pants. "It was right here. Oh well, there's also the phone company. I refuse to pay those rates and they have been slamming me, breaking in on my long distance calls. These people are cheating me."

Mr. Holderead knows how to keep him on target. "Bill, I charge by the hour and this meeting will be expensive. Let's take care of the other business first. I've drawn up a power of attorney naming your daughter, Helen here, in charge. If there is need for a conservator, she will be the one who handles your affairs. We've talked about this and you said these were your wishes."

Dad looks at the table. "Yes, I did say that. I hope it won't be necessary, but someone should be in charge. I guess I'll sign it."

He carefully reads the document again, takes the ballpoint pen out of his pocket, clicks the pen down, hovers over the line, and carefully signs his name. As he finishes, I hear my breath as I fully exhale. I breathe in again and the tension in my chest relaxes and the tight space between my shoulder blades softens.

I now have the responsibility of handling his affairs and to be his conservator should he be judged incompetent. The Conservatorship gives me the right to take charge of his medical and financial decisions.

I walk out with my legs trembling. If I had known then what I had just agreed to manage I might have protested even more than my dad did. I didn't know that he had twenty checking accounts in three different names all over the country, not to mention an assortment of stock and bonds. He gives diversification a bad name.

We return to the house and Dusty begins the awesome task of sorting through Dad's papers. There are at least six rooms filled with boxes. Dusty finds old magazines, old love letters between Dad and Mom, and letters to and from Dad and his brother and sister, unpaid bills and uncashed checks. Some of the papers are important and need to go to the accountant so Dad can file three years of delinquent taxes. They are all mixed together randomly in different boxes and rooms.

Watching Dusty handle his papers is upsetting to Dad. He grabs a plastic bag and places a couple of letters and bank statements in there. "See," he yells, "I know what I'm doing. Leave my stuff alone."

To distract him, I talk Dad into going to the bedroom with me. We need to pack for his trip to California. He gives me a pair of shoes. They are size 13 and take up the entire suitcase. "Dad, your feet are so big we will need a separate suitcase for each of your shoes." He forgets he's upset and laughs. I look in his closet and he has five pairs of running shoes exactly the same. "Anything else you need?"

"Just a minute," he says and takes off downstairs to the basement. I hear the familiar sound of his big feet hitting the stairs. This is one of the last times I will hear the thumping as he takes the steps two at a time. A wave of sadness washes over me. I haven't felt this grief since Mom died. I remember the night when Billy, Dusty, Dad and I returned from the hospital. Dad hung her coat up in the front closet and then took her nightgown to the laundry room to wash later. I didn't say anything to him…like Mom is dead and you don't need to hang her coat up or wash her nightgown. I watched him, struck by his lack of consciousness that she wasn't going to be around to wear those clothes anymore.

The last footstep echoes and Dad enters the bedroom yelling: "You should see what Dusty is doing. He's ruining my things." He runs up to Dusty and pushes him. "You dummy, stop it."

I'm scared to see my father being so physical, but I'm also outraged that he is denigrating my little brother. He's come here because he loves Dad. "Don't you ever call my brother a dummy again.. He's trying to help."

Dusty smiles at me gratefully. "Maybe I should get out of here and return the VCRs. For some reason Dad went to Wal-Mart the month before and bought four TVs and four VCRs. They're still in boxes in the living room."

"Can Dusty use your charge card to get credit for the merchandise?"

"He doesn't know what he's doing. I better go with him. He's a …"

I look at Dad with hard eyes and tight lips. He stops his sentence. I can visualize the scenario. Dad and Dusty are at the check out line at Wal-Mart. Dad forgets that he has agreed to return the equipment and thinks he is being cheated and begins fighting Dusty.

"Let's not worry about the TVs and VCRs now. You and I need to finish packing. Maybe, we should call some of your friends, like Irma and Milt, and Betty Fleck and Grant Russell and say goodby to them. Don't you think?"

"Alright."

Dusty goes to the basement, hoping to be out of sight as he sorts through more of Dad's things. Dad and I have brief conversations with Irma and Betty. They ask about David, my daughter Myrrhia and step-son Aaron, and let me know that they are sorry that I'm not staying longer but understand. Dad doesn't have much to say. "How was that, to say good by?" I ask him.

"Not too bad. They've been telling me that I should go with you. Everyone seems to think that they need to take care of me. I really don't like it."

Dusty must have come back up the stairs quietly because I don't hear him enter the room. "You both still up? I'm tired and am going to bed."

"Me too," I'm exhausted. "How about you Dad?"

"No I have too much to do."

I'm awakened to some rustling sounds. I hope it isn't a mouse. I gingerly open the door to the living room. The light is on and Dad has spread out the papers Dusty had sorted. "What's going on?" I ask.

"I have some chocolate downstairs. Do you want some?"

Great. Now he really is manic--Effexor plus chocolate. He is walking around in his underwear. His fly is open and I can see his penis, but he doesn't seem to have any awareness of exposing himself. He has a wild look in his eyes and I'm wary of him. "No thanks, Dad. What are you doing?"

"Dusty has messed up everything and lost my important papers. I'm taking these to California where he can't touch them. He is so stupid."

"He's not stupid. Take whatever you want." My body feels heavy and my exhale which starts as a sigh, ends up with me beginning to cry.

"What's wrong Helen?"

"It's two in the morning and I guess I'm just tired. I need to go to bed."

"I'm sorry but you know how it is sometimes."

"Yes, Dad, I'm beginning to learn how it is sometimes. Please don't eat any more chocolate tonight."

My worries for my dad started when Billy was twelve, I was ten, and Dusty was seven years old. We were beginning a family vacation, a drive across the country from Indiana to California. Dad shared the ownership of three retail stores with his mother and brother. We stopped in Chicago while Dad did some buying for the stores and Mom took us to the Museum of Science and Industry and Marshall Fields. I had never been in a department store before and this had the largest selection of toys I had ever seen. I bought a wind-up train that followed a track. Watching it follow the same route repetitively became boring. However, it was useful later as a prop to deliver dolls to town so they could go shopping or work as secretaries.

The second day of the vacation we returned to the hotel and found a note that Dad had collapsed and was in the hospital. Mom started crying and yelling for someone, anyone, to call him there immediately. For some reason she thought the desk clerk was too slow finding our room key. The bellman responding to her distress or wanting to keep her quiet, opened the door to our room, dialed the telephone and handed it to her. She quickly left with him to secure a cab, leaving my brothers and me in the hotel room.

My mother's father had died when she was 10-years-old. She didn't talk about it much, but I knew that her life was changed forever. They lost their money, her older brother became what we called at that time a "hood". Mom said that he pawned the family jewelry when he was 14-years-old. Why he did such a thing, what he needed with the money, I never asked.

I thought about how Mom was my age when she lost her dad and began to cry. Billy told me to shut up as he and Dusty watched TV. I laid on the bathroom floor and quietly wept, with only the cold tile against my face to comfort me.

Dad had to stay in the hospital for a couple of days, and Mom stayed in Chicago with him. So Dusty, Billy and I took the train back to our home in Marion, Indiana.

We'd had a trial run a few years before. Mom had been afraid that rail travel would become extinct, and she wanted us to experience it so she bought Billy and me a train ticket from Huntington to Ft. Wayne Indiana, a 45 minute ride. She put us on the train and drove to Ft. Wayne and was there when we got off. This time, Billy and I were experienced train passengers and neither afraid nor that excited by the trip.

Dusty and Billy sat together and played with plastic animals. Dusty's bear slowly approached Bill's lion which would suddenly jump and try to maul the bear. I sat in the seat behind them and watched. I was scared about Dad and wished my mom were there to reassure me that he was strong and would be fine. I wanted her to tell me that even though her dad had died, he wasn't like mine. After all, my dad ate only healthy foods, avoided fats or sugar, never drank coffee, rarely drank alcohol, and exercised. He ran up and down the stairs at the store. Of course, my dad wouldn't die.

A lady who had gray hair and looked like somebody's grandmother walked down the aisle and saw me alone. She sat down and asked me my name and if I wanted a cookie. Suddenly, Dusty and Billy were interested and turned around to watch. I knew it was okay to tell her my name, but I wasn't certain about taking the cookie. Billy announced that he was my brother and so was Dusty and they liked cookies. So each of us took one, but I watched them eat theirs first to ensure the treats weren't poisoned. Anyway, I liked to eat my desserts really slow so that Billy's would be gone and I could see him eye my ice cream cone or chocolate pudding as I savored each lick.

The scenery from the train window was the same relentless green fields of soybeans or cows or corn. Thankfully, the lady asked me questions, so I told her about Dad being in the hospital and that my Aunt Barbara was meeting us at the station. I also told her that until Mom came home I would probably stay with my cousin Alice.

She showed me pictures of her grandchildren, which gave me something else to think about.

A couple of days later Dad returned to Marion; and by that weekend he'd recovered, so we resumed the vacation. From Indiana to California and back is a long drive, especially with three rambunctious children. Mom sang us silly songs and made up stories in which my brothers and I took turns being the major characters, or sometimes the entire family's identities were thinly disguised. But we soon we tired of the songs and the tales and began teasing and hassling each other. At times our fighting and arguing in the back seat escalated to the point that Dad stopped the car and instructed us to get out and as he put it: "run it off". He drove the car slowly for us to follow. Since Billy was stronger and could hit harder, my goal was not only to outrun him, but to keep up with the car so I could talk to Dad through the front window.

During the first part of the drive my brothers and myself had two concerns-- when we would stop at the next Howard Johnsons for ice cream and finding a motel with a swimming pool. Mom wanted to make reservations ahead, but Dad refused, so sometimes we drove far into the night until we found a room. While Mom and the boys slept in the back seat, I sat up front with Dad. We didn't talk but I enjoyed the stars, the white car lights on the pavement, and the quiet hum of the motor. The next day, he would concede to our demands and either stop at a town with a public pool or book us into a motel where we could stop in the late afternoon for a swim. Finally, we reached Utah and Colorado. I loved the light and colors reflecting off the granite walls and the clear mountain rivers and lakes. Swimming pools and ice cream became less important. We visited the Grand Canyon and I wanted to hike to the bottom. I didn't understand that most people don't hike down and out in one day, and I started running down the trail. Dad had to bring me back.

One day Mom and I walked alone along the beach in Carmel, and she told me how scared she'd been when Dad collapsed. Despite her irritation with his refusal to make motel reservations, she said that she thought he was a wonderful man and would miss him terribly if he died. She offered her hand to me, but I refused it, feeling that I was much too old to be seen by anybody holding my mother's hand. She went on talking anyway saying

17

that she'd thought about me while in the hospital, because I was the same age as she had been when her dad died. The cool moist ocean air felt like a damp cloth on my hot forehead and the coarse sand offered itself to my feet, so that I dug into it with each step. I told her about how I had cried on the bathroom floor.

Never being one to enjoy physical exercise, Mom stopped walking and asked me to sit with her. "I know how much you love your father and I'm sorry to have left you, but I needed to be with my him, and someday you'll understand." Somehow I knew what she meant. And on her death bed twenty-three years later, she was explicit when she entrusted Dad to me, like her jewelry and her family silver, with her dying words: "Take care of your dad. He loves you."

The next morning I awaken before Dusty and Dad and decide to go for a run along the river. I take the route through my neighborhood, Shady Hills, remembering when we were the first Jewish family to live in this area. My parents were excited about the house. They came home to tell my brothers and me and asked us for our opinions. Not wanting to leave my school and make new friends; after all, I had just survived junior high and was looking forward to high school, I voted no. My brothers didn't want to make a change either. After we had our say, our parents told us we were moving anyway. At my new high school I was the first Jewish person many of the students had ever known. One of them asked if my family drank blood at Passover. I assured him that the only sacrificial item was a cooked lamb shank. But I loved the new house and enjoyed having my own large room and bathroom, after sharing a little one with four other people. We didn't have money for the first few years for furniture so my parents bought three big pillows. My brothers and I would hold them in front of us and run as fast as we could, trying to knock each other down.

At the end of the lane I smell the familiar freshness of rich moist spring grass and damp earth. The odor of grass is never as rich as it is here. Maybe the first few times we encounter a smell become the prototypes and later variants are disappointing. As I turn the corner I want to wave to the tulips, cheerfully lining the neighbor's walk. Rather than continuing through Shady Hills, I turn left and run by my piano teacher's house to River Road. The corn is just beginning to show its tops, and a light breeze brushes the leaves of the trees standing guard above the river. I run the road to the park, past the tennis courts where I flirted with Billy's friends as I watched him play. When I was a little girl, they had lions in cages in the park. They strolled back and forth, dancing a neurotic tango which marked the dimensions of their confinement. Now I enter the path which follows the Mississinewa River. The rains have been heavy this year, and the river is a huge rushing torrent, which matches the feelings that swell and roll through me. I push on as fast I can until I arrive breathless at the dam. It is open and water rushes out the other side and threatens to overflow the banks. I stand on a narrow piece of cement. On hot summer days when we were young, Dad brought Billy and me here to fish. He told us to be quiet as we stood on a dirt bank and cast our lines, careful to miss the trees. The bobber floated lazily at the end of our bamboo poles. We caught little sunfish that Dad returned to the river.

As I stand there watching the water, I'm filled with a longing for those days, when my only worry was that Billy would try and catch my fish. Sometimes the fish would yank the bobber down and I would pull it up to find an empty hook. Dad patiently dug the barb into another worm, leaving enough of the bait dangling to entice a fish to bite. If Billy then caught a fish I was convinced that he caught the fish that ate my worm and that fish belonged to me. I would yell and cry, scaring any fish in its right mind clean out of that area of the river.

Grief and fatigue overtake me. My heart feels like it's pushing against my throat and my eyes ache. The energy that pushed my legs to turn over quickly, so that the wind blew against my face as I ran is gone. I wonder how much time it will take me to return if I walk. I start back and don't even break into a jog until I'm at the park. After one last long look at the tennis courts, I begin to slowly run. I think about crossing the fields until I find a way to the river and my old hiding place. Dad used to warn me. "Don't go down by the river.

There are bad men down there." Once I saw a puppy hanging by its neck, shot through with bullet holes. This is not a time to tempt fate, so I follow River Road back to the house. Dusty and Dad are in the kitchen having breakfast.

"Did you run?" Dusty asks.

"Kind of." I would like Dusty to ask, "what do you mean by 'kind of'", but he isn't a person who thinks or talks about feelings. If he is having a difficult time, he isn't expressing it..

"Helen," Dad clears his voice. "I'm sorry about last night. I ate too much chocolate and drank some brandy and was carried away. I know that you and Dusty are here to help me."

This is new behavior. My father is a firm believer in moderation. He gave me a book about Benjamin Franklin for my thirteenth birthday that preached the philosophy of the middle road, a watered down version of Aristotle. It was not my most exciting birthday gift that year. This is a great opportunity to pay him back for all those lectures he gave me on correct behavior. I could use one of his favorite lines to me as a child: "Do you think staying up all night drinking brandy and eating chocolate is showing good judgment?" But instead I say: "Thanks Dad. Try to lay off that stuff tonight."

He nods, "Don't worry."

I decide that subject has been dealt with and ask, "Can I have the name of your travel agent? I want to see if we can sit together on the plane home."

"Sure, she is a really great lady. Her name is...Let me look it up for you."

I call her and introduce myself as Dad's daughter.

"Oh yes. Your dad has told me about his children. I've known him for years. We've all been worried about him. I'll call the airlines. They often make special arrangements for situations like these."

Dad has reservations on an earlier flight which is more expensive than mine. At no extra cost she changes my ticket, so that we can fly together. She also notifies the airlines that Dad has Alzheimers and that there might be some trouble.

The next morning Dad is calm. I hope this behavior continues at least until he is on the plane. Dusty will drive us to the Ft. Wayne airport and then stay on for a couple of days in Marion to meet with the accountant, and organize some of Dad's papers.

As we pull away, I look back at the house wondering if I will ever see it again. Without Dad here, I have no reason to return. Although the surrounding communities have grown, the population of Marion has actually decreased. I'm grateful that it hasn't become a strip mall and I'll miss the woods and some of the people, but not the religious prejudice and racial hatred.

The sky is gray and a light rain begins to fall. Dad is talkative, giving Dusty directions to the airport during the 45 minute drive. At the airport he yells that Dusty is placing the bags on the scale incorrectly. The airport attendants give me a knowing look which causes me to wonder if they have been told ahead of his condition and if the computer has a special star for Alzheimers by his name. Before boarding the plane, I hug Dusty goodby. He promises to come to Santa Cruz soon. Then a small prop jet carries us from Fort Wayne to Chicago. During the hour and a half lay over, I order a slice of pizza which arrives swimming in so much grease that I use my napkin to soak it up. Dad spends a long time in the bathroom, and I'm worried about what he is doing in there and whether he'll stay in so long that we will miss our connection. Finally he comes out and we have plenty of time to board the next plane.

About a half an hour into the five hour flight from Chicago to San Jose, Dad begins pacing up and down the aisles. He tries to enter the cockpit and I invite him back to his seat. He sits for about 20 minutes and then begins walking again, hovering outside the curtain where the pilot and co-pilot are guiding the plane. Again I take his hand and guide him back to his seat. So far, so good, but I am worried that he may start to make trouble by wanting to talk with the pilot. The flight attendant walks by and says to me knowingly: "He's wandering now." I say: "Sure," because everyone associates Alzheimers and wandering, but to me he isn't walking aimlessly and lost. He seems anxious, like he doesn't know what to do with himself.

Thankfully, he stays in his seat for a little while but begins talking about the clouds outside the window, the possible fabrics which might have been used to cover the seats, anything that catches his attention at that moment. My usually taciturn father is so loquacious that at one point I beg for some silence and instruct him to look at his magazine. I don't know if he still has the ability to read. He glances at the magazine, turns it over a couple of times and begins walking the aisles again.

We have three more hours before landing. David promised to pick us up at the airport and I wonder what feelings will be stirred up in him. A year ago Larry, his father was hospitalized with cancer and asked to come live with us. David took a similar flight from Ohio to bring him to our house. When he left the hospital, Larry was abruptly taken off morphine, which caused him to be so disoriented that he took off running at the airports. Finally, David tied a rope between he and his father so he wouldn't lose him.

When he came to the house, he asked me to kneel with him and pray. I agreed at first until he started to direct his supplications to the Saint Myrrhia. Its okay to love and adore your granddaughter, but she was no 16-year-old pure form who would deliver him to heaven. Although Larry moved in and out of sanity, most of the time he was cognizant of his death and approached it with fear and dignity. His life review, enabled him to come to terms with himself. David and I stayed with him during his final breaths, as he slowly let go of this world.

Although David respects my father, I wonder how he'll feel about Dad now. Alzheimers is a disease that kidnaps the personality and hides it behind veils.

Sometimes, my dad is there with his grin and large warm hands. Other times, a hostile and aggressive fellow appears, who doesn't know the day of the week. It has taken away my father's capacity for self reflection; and if the disease follows its usual course of decline, he won't be able to be cognizant of his own death.

It is time to serve lunch and the flight attendant instructs Dad to return to his seat. He dismantles his sandwich and begins soaking any juice off the meat, like he had seen me do with the greasy pizza. He works on that piece of meat with his napkin for what seems eternity until I roughly say: "Stop."

I want to be more patient and kind, like I was with Larry, but I am appalled that this man who I admired as the greatest person on earth is engaged in such mindless compulsivity.

He looks at me and says: "I don't think I will ever see my home again."

My chest tightens and my throat aches. I don't want to cause him pain and I also want to continue having a peaceful relationship with him at least during the plane flight, yet I answer truthfully: "Probably not." He says nothing and never mentions the subject of his home again.

PART 2
SUNSHINE VILLA

Dad and I, like so many parents and children of the time, took different stands during the Vietnam war. With two other psychology graduate students, I formed a draft resistance organization at the University.of Wisconsin. I entered the draft board under the guise of doing psychological research and illegally copied the names of the men who were 1A. Then I went to the court house and looked up their addresses and phone numbers. We invited them to a meeting and provided those who were potential resistors with a variety of means to avoid the draft-- information regarding medical or psychological deferments or trips into Canada. My mom and I were on one side, and my dad on the other. Those had been the dividing lines since my teen years. Dad had intimations not to trust the government or the phone company. He gave helpful advice on how to avoid arousing the suspicion of the FBI, so that I never put my name on fliers or discussed any draft resistance business over my telephone in case it was tapped.

"Paranoia runs deep in the heartland." The line from Paul Simon's song, "Have a good time", often plays in my mind during the days my father lives at Sunshine Villa. This assisted living facility sits high on a hill three blocks from the Pacific Ocean. The stately edifice wraps around a city block, holding the top of the hill majestically. Below it are the Boardwalk, the wharf, and Beach flats.

The Boardwalk is known for its amusement rides, especially its hand-painted carousel and antique roller coaster. The first time I rode the roller coaster, I was twenty years old and was with my two brothers. We climbed the first hill and bravely marveled at the sight of the entire city of Santa Cruz on one side and the blue ocean on the other. Suddenly, we were plunged into a series of dips, rises and yanking turns. Tears poured down my cheeks. I could hear Billy saying, "fuck, oh fuck," over and over again, while Dusty pleaded, "no, oh no." Finally we were jerked to a stop. The three of us stared at each other and said in unison, "Let's go again."

Due north of the Boardwalk is the wharf. It is large enough for cars and lined with restaurants so that the smell of grease combines with kelp and fish. Seals hang out on the pilings below and their barking provides a chorus to the waves caressing the shore and the screams from the roller coaster.

Most areas of Santa Cruz are diverse, but the neighborhood where Sunshine Villa resides is particularly extreme in that regard. Marginal apartments are interspersed with stately Victorian homes. In Beach Flats children's voices ring out with a mixture of English and Spanish and it is known as a likely spot to score drugs and find prostitutes.

Dark mahogany doors open to a room with deep mauve carpet. The furniture is old and expensive looking. In the elegant dining room, the residents eat on white linen tablecloths. I ask a well-groomed regal woman how she likes it here. "I am very pleased with this place," she says but then warns me. "Patience is required at Sunshine Villa." I notice that the portions are small and the service is interminably slow. The waiters and waitresses are young and friendly and try their best to please. Perhaps they will help dissipate Dad's frustration at having to wait for his food.

I call Linda, the manager of Sunshine Villa to inform her that Dad will be ready to move in the next day. She tells me: "We have an electrically operated reclining chair that he might try. Men often like gadgets and I wonder if this is something that your dad would be interested in."

"Sure," I say, "he's fascinated by electronic devices."

I take him to see the place and watch for his reaction. Linda introduces us to Dianne, a voluptuous young woman with clear white skin who is in charge of marketing. We follow her down the hall as the skirt of her long cotton dress sways with her walk. She stops at various rooms, explaining the job of each staff member and telling each person about Dad. Aware that he has difficulty remembering, Dad takes a folded piece of paper from his pocket and asks Dianne for a pen or pencil so he can write down the names of everyone he meets. They have plenty of vivacious young women and his chest expands with their attention.

The older women residents all look him over and whisper among themselves. He doesn't seem to notice them. Dianne shows us his apartment. The large windows are dressed with ruffled curtains and the room is light and spacious. A flowered spread covers a single bed and etched glass lamps rest on heavy dark wooden tables.

Each room has its own refrigerator, but residents are not allowed to have stoves as they might forget and burn the place down.

Dad immediately sits in the electrical recliner and adjusts it up and down, forward and back. He has a big grin on his face and says, "Look, I press this button and the chair..." He is thrown back into a reclining position. "Just a minute," and he pulls himself up finds the button which allows him to sit up, but then he is thrown too far forward. He finds the right button and sits up laughing. "Do you want to try it?"

"Not now. I have some things to do at home." I leave him playing with his chair and feeling like I have left a child at his first day at camp. I'm surprised that all has gone so well, but have my doubts as to how long he will be satisfied with a recliner chair.

The first few days are quiet and I begin to allow myself to feel a little relief. We go to lunch and I take him to dinner a couple of times, and he has few complaints. Mainly he wants his car and access to his accounts. Although I don't like his demanding tone, I am still optimistic that maybe this will work. The third day I receive a call.

"Hello, this is Sunshine Villa. Your father is down at the boardwalk and has locked himself in a phone booth. He won't let us in."

"Has he hurt anyone?" I ask.

"No."

"Is he hurt?"

"No. Its just that we knock on the door and he won't let us in."

"Okay," I say. "In a couple of hours I have a break in my schedule and will come over."

I arrive at Sunshine Villa and find Dad in his room. The dark Victorian furniture has been moved against the walls and the bed is now on the floor. The drawers are half open and are full of bananas. Newspapers, fliers, letters, and magazines lie in piles on the floor. The lamp shades are sitting on the lamps, but upside down.

"What's going on?" I ask.

"I want my car," he yells. "I want my checkbook. David has stolen my things."

"How has David stolen your things?"

"He put them in his box and took them. He stole my stuff."

David came over the other night to visit Dad. He brought a box of papers. Dad must have decided that David put his things in there. I am the one who has his driver's license and 15 checkbooks, but it is easier to blame David than to blame me. After all, he always thought David stole his daughter, so why not his checkbook and driver's license too.

"David doesn't have your stuff."

He makes fists of his hands and yells, "You're trying to control me. Let me have my car."

I'm scared and feel like a little girl. Across from me is my father and I want to go to him for comfort and protection, but he is the one yelling at me. I start to cry.

"What's wrong?" he asks.

I say through the tears, "I want my Dad."

"I'm your dad", he says and reaches his arms out to me.

I cry against his chest. I am the adult who took away his car and he is screaming at me like an angry child. He has Alzheimers, yet he's still the

25

parent who wants to protect his daughter. Get a grip, I say to myself, or you will both go crazy.

I decide not to worry about the furniture or the bed. I go home, once more wondering if I am the best person to be in charge of my dad. Maybe Billy or Dusty could manage him better. However, neither of them is willing to deal with Dad on this level. Both Dad and Mom have chosen me to be caretaker, but it has always seemed unfair to me, those sex role divisions. Mom used to say: "A son's a son until he takes a wife, but a daughter's a daughter for the rest of her life."

Chapter 3
The Dementia Group

When I enroll Dad in Sunshine Villa, I am given a list of services for the elderly in Santa Cruz. I call the Live Oak Senior Center to find out what's available for people dealing with Alzheimers. A voice on the answering machine asks for my name and number and promises to call back.

The next day Dolores calls. "Come on down. We have a library with books that might be helpful. Also, we have a group that meets several times a week for caretakers with parents or other family members with dementia."

"I'm not actually living with my dad. He's staying at Sunshine Villa."

"Of course. Most of the people in the group share your situation. Their parents are elsewhere, but they're still the primary caregivers."

I decide to attend the meeting at 7:00 on Tuesday evening at the Live Oak Senior Center. I have been the leader of many therapy and training groups, but haven't been a group member for several years now. We sit on metal folding chairs arranged in a circle. Of the nine members of the group, only two are men. Everyone looks a little haggard. I seem to be the only member from "the sandwich generation", trying to balance children and parents. I wish I didn't have to add work as condiment on the sandwich. Mom always said: "You try to do too much." Then again, maybe I am the only one here with a child still at home because the others with children couldn't even make it to the group. Really, I'm probably a lucky one.

People take turns speaking. One pretty slender woman with gray hair and a soft voice is caring for her mother and father. Both of them are suffering from dementia. She lives alone, can't find people to watch them and doesn't seem to have much of a life. Another woman complains that her mother will only eat canned food even though her brother owns a restaurant and is a gourmet cook. Her mother wants to heat food in pots, and she and her brother are afraid she will forget to turn off the stove and burn the house down. They are trying to teach her how to use a microwave. I remember a phone call from Dad after Dorothy left. He was trying to cook eggs in the microwave and they were exploding. I decide not to share this.

The leaders are aware of our struggle to provide for our dependent parents, without becoming depleted. Time and time again we are reminded to set limits and take care of ourselves. One woman lives with her father who has had a series of strokes. She is quite thin and I notice that I am beginning to lose weight myself from the stress. Her father is hostile with

27

her and his other caretakers. She is afraid to leave the house, to leave him alone. He continually asks after his wife. He forgets that she is dead and his daughter tells him again and again. One of the group leaders says: "Why are you torturing him like that? He won't remember. Tell him she will be back in awhile." The leader's words shock me. The last thing this woman wants to do is torture her father. I don't know the whole story. Maybe the leader has confronted her before on this matter, or maybe the leader herself recently lost a husband and doesn't want to be continually reminded. The group is silent for awhile.

Another woman begins to speak. Her square face matches her square body. I always think of women like that as the kind who volunteer to lead the girl scout troop, always bring a nice dish to the potluck and have a van filled with five or six children. But then I take another look, notice the lines on her face and a few silver hairs and realize those days are past and her children are probably grown. She has a mother who has lived in several different residential facilities and for the last few years has been residing in a care home in Salinas. They've removed all the phones because the residents are dialing 911. She states this fact without much concern. However, she is worried about her mother's teeth. She has dentures and the few teeth she has left are rotting because there is no one to brush them. Her mother is also disappearing to the point that she barely recognizes her, her own daughter. She decides her mother's teeth aren't that important. Her shoulders sink back against the chair and the lines smooth out on her face. I don't even want to think about the day my dad wouldn't recognize me or have to watch his teeth turn brown and fall out. I decide right there and then to have his teeth checked. I was glad that he had his missing tooth fixed.

When I return home, David is lying in bed reading. He looks up from his journal and asks about the meeting.

"It was great to sit in a room with people dealing with similar issues and hear about the same feelings I've experienced. It's incredible to me that the county provides such a service. I'd like to go back sometime soon. They've got a library too and a list of care facilities. I checked out this book, The Thirty-six Hour Day."

"Quite a title. Want a glass of wine?"

"Sure."

"Blair called. I told her you were at the meeting. She wanted to know how you're doing and Rebecca Campbell wants to know if you can meet her for dinner Thursday night."

"Is that okay with you?"

"Of course, you need your friends."

While David goes to the kitchen to pour me my favorite evening drink, a glass of white wine with raspberries, I call Blair. She has been checking on me regularly since my dad started having Alzheimers. Her mother died from the disease and I'd asked her if it wasn't difficult to listen to me. She said that it helped her to talk about it, because nobody at the time had truly comprehended what she was dealing with. After attending that meeting, I understood what she meant.

She answers the phone with her characteristic: "Hello, the Bashford residence." I wonder if she does that because she is a woman living alone and wants someone to think otherwise.

"Hi Blair. It's me."

"How was the meeting?" I can picture her round even featured face. Blair is one of the most attentive people I know and one of the smartest.

"It was good. A woman talked about her mom beginning to not recognize her."

Blair sighs. "I remember those times."

"I bet you do. That must have been hard. What bothered her the most was her mother's teeth rotting. I'm making sure that doesn't happen to my dad."

"Do you want to take that on?" Blair has a different philosophy of life than mine. She lives alone because she doesn't want to hassle with people. The course of least resistance is her way, while It's easier for me to do battle than remain passive.

"Yes. I need to do this."

"Well, I know you're busy with your father, but I'd like to refer you a client."

"It depends, I like the distraction, but I don't want to take on anything too heavy."

David brings me the wine and I pantomime a kiss.

Just then I hear my 17-year-old daughter Myrrhia call from her bedroom across the hall, "I have a friend who needs help."

"Just a minute Myrrhia. I'll be right there. Tell me about the client Blair."

Myrrhia comes and stands in the hallway. Listening to Blair's description with Myrrhia standing by the phone waiting is somewhat distracting. I wave her back into her room, while telling Blair, "sure have her call me." I then stand at the door to Myrrhia's room. She has painted her small room, latrine green which makes it appear even smaller. Posters cover all the walls, from Bob Marley to Albert Einstein. Interspersed are pictures of her friends, her brother, Aaron, one photo of me and David, and cards. CDs and tapes scatter the floor, and when the light is out, the ceiling glows with fluorescent stars. Her desk is piled with purses, books, and papers and the cat has claimed the desk chair as her own. In all this chaos she manages to produce good grades and is organized about her assignments.

"What's up?"

She looks up from her book. Long brown curls frame an oval face that Modigliani would have loved to paint.

"Dylan is so depressed that he's talking about killing himself. I don't know what to do."

What about his parents?"

"He lives with his mom and he's angry at her. He wants you to be his therapist."

I know this young man. He's followed me around at Myrrhia's parties. Several of the boys have a habit of hovering near me, trying to get my attention, while the girls seem to be more direct about telling me what concerns them. I agree with Myrrhia that Dylan needs help. Since I can't take him on as a patient because of their friendship, I give her a list of names of other therapists. "How are you doing?" I ask her.

"Fine. I'm reading Barbara Kingsolver, <u>The Bean Tree.</u> What a good book." She begins to analyze the text, but I stop her.

"I'm tired. Let's talk tomorrow". I write a note to call my dentist to make an appointment for Dad and then gratefully undress for bed.

Lift Line is picking up Dad at Sunshine Villa and taking him to the dentist's office and then back to Sunshine Villa. Thank goodness for all of these services. On the morning of his dental appointment, I'm meeting with a new client. He's in his thirties, married and has two young children. The problem is that his wife has multiple sclerosis. Over the last five years he has watched her change from a competent, active working woman and mother, to being confined at home in a wheel chair. His plan had always been to live in Santa Cruz by the beach and have a carefree existence. His wife wants to move to a safer neighborhood and the new house needs to be refitted to treat her handicap. Instead of selecting tile or carpet for their new home, they're placing handle guards on the showers and installing low cabinets in the kitchen.

After he departs, I find myself staring out the window. The nasturtiums along the fence seem uncommonly orange, so bright they almost hurt my eyes. Dealing with my father's disease seems mild in comparison to what this man faces. After all, Dad has lived many years full of rewarding and interesting experiences, and we all must die. But this man's wife is young, a mother, and the illness is changing his life in such a way that it seems to be tearing at the fabric of his dreams.

My office phone has a loud annoying ring and I'm startled by the sound. "Hello, it's Doreen from Dr. Brennan and Dr. Coffee's office. Sorry to bother you. Your dad's visit turned out great." She pauses and then continues in her sweet voice, "but he won't leave."

I hear a gruff voice say: "Let me talk to her."

She says, "Joe wants to talk to you."

Joe is the Lift Line driver, and I hear the frustration in his voice. "Your father refuses to come with me. I have other people to drive. He won't listen to me."

"Let me talk to Dad."

"'Hi Helen," Dad says with excitement. "How are you?"

"Fine. I'm here working."

"Listen, I need to go to Wal-Mart."

"But Dad, there is no Wal-Mart in Santa Cruz."

"I know. I understand," he says with assurance. "I want to go to the Wal-Mart in Indianapolis."

"Indianapolis is 2,000 miles away. It's in Indiana. You're in California."

"Helen, I know perfectly well where I am and I know that Indianapolis is only an hour away."

"It's an hour away from Marion."

"I don't need your help. I can hitch hike there."

"Just a minute. Let me talk to Doreen."

"Hi," Doreen says calmly. I see her black curly hair and full red lips. "Your dad is sweet and doing so well."

"Right," I say. "Could you please tell Joe to go ahead and someone will be there for Dad shortly. And please tell Dad to wait." I'm pleading.

"Oh, not to worry," she says. "Joe already left."

I try to calm myself. I have clients and can't get too upset. I try deep breathing. "Do I cancel my appointments and retrieve Dad? How will I convince him to go back to Sunshine Villa?"

Just then, Myrrhia walks down the hall. She is a slender 5 feet 7 inches tall with large firm breasts and grace that comes from years of ballet and feeling like she belongs on this planet. She smiles that smile that lights up the world and says: 'How's it going Mom?"

"Grandpa is at the dentist's office and won't leave. He wants to go to Wal-Mart. I guess I will have to cancel my clients and go get him."

"What are you going to do? Take him to Wal-Mart in San Jose?"

"I'm not taking him to Wal-Mart. Besides he wants to go to the one in Indianapolis."

"Mom. I can handle this."

"What are you going to do?"

"Don't worry. Besides, I heard your client come in. You better go." She kisses me on the cheek. "Go."

31

An hour passes. I'm ready to meet the next client when I notice Myrrhia in her room. "How did it go?" I ask her.

"Fine."

"What did you do?"

"I went to the dentist's office. I said: 'Let's go Grandpa.' He got in the car. I drove him to Sunshine Villa. He says that he feels like he is your puppy and you have him on a chain. I didn't say anything to that. When we arrived at Sunshine Villa he said: 'I have to get out here.' I said 'yes.' I told him that you will visit him later."

"That's it?"

"Yeah. That's it. Should there be more?"

I give her a big hug. "Thank you Myrrhia. I love you so much."

As she walks into her bedroom she flashes me a grin and says: "Don't worry Mom. I'm here for you."

The dentist tells me that Dad needs extensive work and he outlines a treatment plan. I ask him to write it down in case there's a question of how much money is to be spent. Dad needs some teeth pulled in order to make a bridge and we are referred to an endodontist. I take two hours from work and go to Sunshine Villa to pick him up. He isn't happy about going to the dentist but after some persuading agrees. We arrive and are given a clipboard with the standard history form to complete. The nurse says that Dad has to fill it out. I whisper to her that might not be possible as he is having some memory problems. "Those are the rules," she responds, tight lipped.

"What's the matter?" Dad asks.

"Nothing, how are you doing?"

"I'm having trouble with some of these questions. It must be my glasses."

"Let me see. Maybe I can help."

"Really Helen? You can answer these questions?"

"Well, some of them."

"What was your dentist's name in Marion?"

"You know them. They have a son who lives in Kokomo and their daughter was friends with you."

"I don't remember being friends with anyone whose father was a dentist."

"Maybe it was Dusty. Dusty's friend."

"Don't worry. I can call Dorothy and find out." We work together and fill out much of the form. It takes about a half hour, jogging Dad's memory. After placing the questionnaire on the ledge by the receptionist's station, I look at some magazines and then check my watch. An hour has passed and

I need to return to work and Dad is getting hungry. I ask the receptionist how long it will be before he sees the dentist.

"Oh, we'll call your dad into the office in about an hour. The dentist visit will probably last half an hour."

"Wait a minute. Our appointment was at 10:30 and it's now 11:30 and you say it will be another hour to an hour and a half. I need to go to work. Is it okay if I go grab us some lunch, and then come back for Dad afterwards?"

"You can't leave him here unattended. We won't be responsible for people in his condition."

"You expect us to sit here and wait two and a half hours for an appointment? That's ridiculous."

"You can't leave."

"And why not?"

"You haven't filled out the back side of the questionnaire."

I look up at her in disbelief. I would like to punch her in her tight lipped, hair sprayed face. Instead I say: "Dad let's go."

"Why Helen? Did I mess up the questionnaire?"

"No, it isn't you. Let's find another endodontist."

"My teeth are fine. I really don't need this surgery."

"I'll take you back to Sunshine Villa. You can have some lunch."

"What about you? Aren't you hungry?"

Except for the few times I have gone out to eat with Dad, I've been skipping lunch. There aren't enough hours in the day. "No I'm fine. I need to get back to work."

At the next meeting of the dementia group I tell them of my experience with the endodontist. Everyone else has been wonderful. John Gillette, his psychiatrist understands and doesn't keep him waiting. At Erik's Deli Dad shouts his order, demanding no fat on the meat or croutons on his salad. He says the same thing every time. I wonder if a list could be compiled of people friendly to demented citizens. The leader says that I have been fortunate. My experiences have been abnormally positive and they aren't allowed to make such claims about anyone in the community.

I tell the dentist what happened with the endodontist and suggest that he shouldn't refer anyone with dementia or a working brain to him again. I am given another referral and arrange for Dad to go on the lift line. That day when I return from my clients, I see the flickering light on my answering machine. It's the receptionist from the endodontist's office. Dad never showed up for the appointment. I call Sunshine Villa and find out that he refused to board the lift line. A reasonable person would probably give up at this point. After all, it's only teeth we are talking about here. He's 82-years-old and who knows, his teeth may outlast his brain, anyway. Sadly, it's not in my nature to easily acknowledge defeat. I make another appointment with Dr. Steel, the endodontist and this time take Dad to his office. What a surprise. The receptionist, Nancy is warm and friendly. I don't have to fill out a health form because she faxed it to me ahead of time. We're taken right in for the appointment. Dr. Steel is a sparkly man with a winning smile and relaxed manner. As luck would have it, he went to dental school at Indiana University with Dad's dentist from Marion. They share stories and Dad becomes his charming self. His teeth will be fixed. We only have to schedule the surgery, so that I can be around to take care of him afterwards.

The next day I pick him up at Sunshine Villa to take him to lunch. I tell him that we have an errand first.

"Sure. An errand to take care of you. I don't get out much. I don't want to do your errand."

"Let's see Dad, you might."

I stop at the gas station and load up the tank. Dad wants to pay for me with his credit card. I start to argue and then remember that he needs to feel useful and in charge. With a full tank of gas I head for the free car wash. As we enter the tunnel, warm moist air sucks out the cool fresh outside air, and huge rubber strips start beating on the car. I feel claustrophobic. The water comes out in a gush and I put my hand on Dad's. "Thanks for coming with me. I don't like being in here alone."

"Why not?"

"It reminds me of dangerous times driving in the Santa Cruz mountains when I couldn't see out of the windshield."

Dad has a large grin on his face. He loves mechanical devices. "I'm sorry I said I didn't want to go. That was fun. Thank you."

Around the corner is Erik's Deli, the closest thing to a Jewish delicatessen in Santa Cruz. I thought he might like a corned beef sandwich. Standing in line isn't a concept that makes sense to him, so he walks in front of the others and gives his order in a demanding voice, "corned beef and salad with no croutons." As she writes, he reminds her as if in 30 seconds she might have forgotten, "no croutons."

The sandwich comes on dark pumpernickel rye with no mayonnaise, huge thick slices of corned beef and the salad has no croutons. He turns his attention to the food and doesn't talk much.

After lunch I ask Dad if he wants to walk next door to "Sees Candy Store".

"You bet," he says. A woman with thick gray hair and a glowing smile asks us if we would like a piece of chocolate. I agree with Dad about trimming fat from meat, but I count chocolate as one of the good fats and think that it should be listed as a major food group. We each take a piece of candy and a sweet blissful smile appears on Dad's face. Slowly, he swallows the last bite and while looking around the store notices that they have boxes of candy that can be shipped. He walks over and examines each selection slowly, then turns to me and says: "Milt Maidenberg would like a box of these candies."

"Of course," I say in total agreement. Every time I visited the Maidenbergs, Milt always offered me a piece of candy, not just any candy but good chocolates. Now he's sick and dying at home, and his wife Irma is taking care of him. When Dad was still in Marion, Milt called him every other day to check on him. Dad buys the box and the woman at Sees agrees to ship it for him. Luckily, I remember Milt and Irma's address.

A week later we receive a thank you note from Irma. It says that Milt died the day before he received it. I'm worried about how Dad will handle this news. When I tell him, his response is: "I think Irma will like that we remembered her and I know their guests will enjoy the chocolates."

That night David and I are at a restaurant celebrating our twentieth wedding anniversary. His face is animated as he explains the findings of a Scientific American article he read. "They've found a way to reverse sound waves when people speak."

"Wait a minute." Sometimes the way David communicates is ambiguous and confusing. "They haven't found a way to take the waves and push them back into people's mouths."

"No they can't do that, but they can change the waves."

He is not contributing information, so I add, "this must be something about surgery."

"Yes," he says excitedly, "do you want me to explain it to you?"

"No, that's okay." I look at his face and wonder if his high cheekbones and delicate features were gifts from his Sioux grandmother. His eyes seem brown but I know that is an illusion. When I look at them carefully, they are blue around the iris, then brown, and finally outlined in green. My mind travels to previous anniversaries and I have an image of his taut body lying inside a grass hut on the island of Bora Bora. My open palm is resting on his forearm and I let it glide up and down his arm, enjoying the feel of coarse yet soft hairs.

"What are you thinking about?" he asks.

"Tahiti. I was remembering languid afternoons of slow love making."

"That was a great anniversary. You ended up accidentally running around the island, completing a marathon, and then swimming in between those islands…."

"What are you talking about? You learned to wind surf, coming in with that big grin on your face and your legs all cut up and bloody."

"Yes, but great sex. Helen, if anyone told me I was to have twenty four years of this kind of lovin…" The wide grin on his face turns to a frown as he hears his cell phone ring."

"Don't answer it."

"It might be Myrrhia." He picks it up. "Hello David here." His face looks concerned. "No honey, you did the right thing. Don't worry. Mom and I will take care of it. We love you." He puts down the phone and says: "That was Myrrhia. She says Sunshine Villa called. Your dad has taken over the laundry room."

"What does that mean, taken over the laundry room?" I call the front desk and find out that Dad has locked everyone out and is doing his wash. David and I hurriedly pay the bill and drive over to Sunshine Villa.

I knock on the door of the laundry room. "Dad, it's Helen and David. Let us in." He can't hear well so I bang and pound on the door.

He opens it part way and I see his head. "Helen and David. What a pleasant surprise. Just a minute while I open the door." He opens it all the way and I see him standing there, dressed only in his underwear. He locks the door behind us. "It's hard to get things done here. I'm trying to wash my clothes but they keep bothering me."

"Dad, do you have any pants?"

David chimes in. "You need to put on some pants, Bill."

"Let me see. I have a pair somewhere. Oh here they are, fresh out of the dryer and nice and clean."

"Please put them on Dad."

"Oh sure." He puts on his pants.

"How about unlocking the door."

"Let me put my clothes in the dryer first. I can't get anything done. They bother me here." I watch as he slowly examines each item of clothing and places it in the machine to be dried. He then walks over and unlocks the door.

That night I dream that Dad lives on a tropical island. There are no cars and no roads so if he takes off he can't go far. He has a house by the ocean. I see him walking in the warm water with his pants legs rolled up. An old woman says his name and offers him some food from a pot. He eats and a big smile comes over his face.

Chapter 4
Psychiatric Evaluation

Following Dr. Hendrie's suggestion, I arrange for Dad to have a psychiatric evaluation. Dad loved the Effexor as he had great bursts of energy and needed little sleep. My assessment that Dad might be manic didn't seem too far off. However, Dr. Hendrie's recommendation that Dad be placed on Risperdal concerns me. It is one of the new classes of antipsychotics that is supposed to help some of the distorted thinking of Alzheimers. I know about anti psychotics. These drugs produce side effects, dry mouth, Parkinsonian symptoms, and finally "the thorazine shuffle", the customary gait of schizophrenics. In fact many schizophrenics go off the drugs. They know their illness will return, but the side effects feel like alien irritants who have invaded their physical bodies to torment them. I want my father to be reasonable and manageable, but I don't like the idea of placing him on one of these drugs.

I call Dr. John Gillette, a psychiatrist who is the expert in our community for treating the elderly. His answering machine says he isn't taking new patients for the next three months, but because I'm a colleague, I'm able to secure an appointment. He also agrees to accept Dad's Medicare insurance as payment; which is generous of him.

I decide to make the appointment a pleasant outing. Afterwards I'll take him to a good restaurant and have a steak dinner. This might assuage any bad feelings he has resulting from the visit.

John's office is on the second floor of an old house in downtown Santa Cruz. It isn't fancy, and I feel comfortable. Like Dad, John is a tall man. His dark skin contrasts with his silver hair, and his blue eyes convey warmth and acceptance. He extends his arm to Dad, they shake hands and we each take a seat. He asks Dad if he has ever seen a psychiatrist before. Dad answers: "Oh yes, for my first born son. He was so difficult my wife and I didn't know what to do. He continually screamed and threw his food on the floor."

John answers softly, "Hmm, threw his food on the floor" and gives me a look.

I think his look is saying what I am thinking, that throwing food isn't unusual behavior for a baby, but Dr. Gillette doesn't know Billy. Mom and Dad always indicated that he was a difficult child. I wonder if I ever threw food on the floor.

"Did the psychiatrist help you?"

"Yes he did, but we only saw him for a short time."

"Do you know why you're here?"

"Yes. It's about my forgettery. That's what I call my memory. It doesn't work too well these days."

"I hear you have been having problems and have come to Santa Cruz with Helen."

"That's right."

"Do you know what day it is?"

"I'm not sure. I think Thursday. The days are all the same to me."

"What season?"

"I think it's the fall."

Dr. Gillette ignores that Dad doesn't know what day it is, but responds to his mistake about the season: "It's June, summer, but the seasons all seem to run together in Santa Cruz, with the fog and all. It's different from the Midwest." He then pulls out a test. It is called the Bender Gestalt and consists of figures--for example a triangle, a line touching a circle, etc. that the person is required to copy. From the results an IQ estimate is possible as well as a diagnosis for emotional issues.

My father has difficulty drawing the first line. He folds the paper and tries to sight from its edge to make a straight line. His illness seems to interfere with his ability to perform this task much more than I would have expected. I mean he doesn't know what day it is or season, but not to be able to draw a straight line is an indication of serious cognitive impairment. His compulsivity won't let him stop the task and he continually tries to line up the piece of paper. I can't stand to watch him struggle and finally take the paper away. I joke. "I guess you're not going to be an architect."

John looks at me and laughs softly. "Yes, you're not going to be an architect." He talks about how his father is 85-years-old, and like my father is quite physically healthy. But his father is still functioning intellectually. I don't want to hear about how well his dad is doing.

John also suggests that we try Dad on Risperdal and writes a prescription. He gives it to me and says: "Hopefully this will help the confusion and not add to it."

So, now I have to convince my dad to take this medication that may help his confusion, or make it worse and has side effects that scare me. Dad has refused to take anything but vitamins his entire life. His mother never gave him candy before the age of twelve. The top of his bureau was covered with articles about the health risks of cigarette smoke. Once in while, he had a social drink. He never drank coffee, avoided fats, fried food or white bread. Even after the car accident, when he and Dorothy were rear-ended at a stop light and he had severe whiplash, even then, he wouldn't take an aspirin. Dad believes that the car accident caused his Alzheimers and maybe he is right. However, if the inflammation from the accident contributed to the Alzheimers, anti-inflammatories or aspirin might have helped. Regardless of the etiology of his dysfunction, I'm now supposed to convince him to take Risperdal. I was on a debate team in high school and college, so I begin to develop my argument.

The sun is bright coming in the windows on the stair landing at Sunshine Villa. Dad is standing, while I sit on the floor looking up at him. David stands next to me on the step below. I try to speak slowly which is not my favorite conversational speed. "Plaques and tangles are forming in your brain. There's a drug called Risperdal that both Dr. Hendrie and Dr. Gillette think might help you. This drug increases the neurotransmitters between the nerve synapses and helps alleviate the symptoms of Alzheimers."

Dad massages his head. "I have funny feelings in my head. I also have tingling in my fingers. What do you think it is?"

"Bill, I'm not sure," David answers him. "You've had a thorough physical."

"Maybe I have arthritis."

"That could be, but if so, it's not serious."

"I rub my fingers." He shows us by massaging each of the fingers on his hands. I study them and can't believe these are the hands of a man in his eighties. The skin is smooth and soft. I don't see any signs of inflammation or swelling of the joints.

"That's good Bill, but what do you think of what Helen is saying about the medication?"

"She worries too much and has some wild ideas. I don't know about this medication."

I 'm feeling desperate but try to calm myself. I stopped asking Dad for help with my math in sixth grade because I was so frustrated with his plodding explanations. When I needed help with one of those story problems involving time, he would begin talking about clocks in general. I became so impatient that I would storm off to the kitchen to my mother.

I see Mom standing at the sink in the kitchen. It was one of the first prefabricated houses, one bathroom for two adults and three children. The kitchen is small and narrow, part of a circle. We can begin running in the living room, go through the kitchen into my bedroom and with a short stint through the hall be back in the living room. She is drying dishes. "He is so slow with his explanations," I complain. "I can't take it."

"I'm not good with math, Helen. Your father is the smart one. He loves you." She would never criticize him. She wasn't the smart one. What a joke. I found out later she'd had a scholarship to a high school for gifted

39

children and was president of her stock club. The fifties was such a wonderful time for women. She always made herself less than my father. But she could convince him to do what she wanted, keep him in line. When she took a stand, she relentlessly pressed her point, never giving up. I'm trying to relate to my father differently, but for the first time am able to see that her strategy had its merits.

Once again, I present the same arguments, how this drug will help his brain process information. Dad's eyes narrow and he looks at David. "Do you think she is right?"

David clears his throat. As he crosses his arms grabbing his left elbow with his right hand, I notice that his hairs stand up and shine gold. "This is Helen's field of expertise and I think you should listen to her."

I look up again at Dad. The light from the window casts a nimbus around his head. "Okay," he says, "if you and David think it's all right, I'll try this medication."

Chapter 5
Father's Day

My brothers are coming down with their families for Father's Day. I've made a reservation for the buffet at Chaminade, Dad's favorite place. This elegant retreat center sits on a hill about two miles from my house. The buffet is served in a large room with plenty of windows that look out over Monterey Bay.

This Father's Day happens to be one of the worst days for traffic in Santa Cruz, as it coincides with UCSC graduation. Billy and Dusty arrive with their families a little late, but they don't complain. Dad is dressed in a suit and excited.

Myrrhia's cousins will be here. Though I've been upset and scared by Dad's temper tantrums and outbursts, she seems to take his behavior in stride. Her cousins haven't seen him for awhile, and I wonder how they will react to Grandpa's strange behavior.

We all sit at one long table. Dad is going back and forth to the buffet, filling his plate up with more and more food. Michael, Dusty's nine-year-old son has also dressed up. He's wearing a blue sports jacket and a white shirt. His brown hair is sticking straight up and his blue eyes are wide and laughing. He whispers to Myrrhia and points to Dad who is walking back to the table carefully balancing a large plate laden with a chocolate brownie, a piece of chocolate pie, a small piece of tiramasu, a slice of key lime pie, a chocolate eclair, a butterscotch brownie, three different kinds of cookies, all topped by a scoop of vanilla ice cream with chocolate sauce. Myrrhia nudges me. I look at Dad and raise my eyebrows.

Billy says: "Helen, should we let him do that?"

Dusty answers: "He's like a kid. We should stop him."

I say: "He's not a kid."

"You try to stop him," adds Billy.

But when Dad tries to fill up a second dessert plate, Billy walks over and steers him away from the table.

"Why?" asks Dad.

"It's time to go," says Bill.

Later that week, I'm aroused from sleep at 3:00 am by the sound of the phone. I hear my father's enraged voice.

41

"They won't serve me breakfast. They're starving me." I count the days since he began the Risperdal. Even if it's going to work, there hasn't been enough time for it to kick in.

"Dad, it's three o'clock in the morning."

"It's 3:00 o'clock at your house, but here it's breakfast time, and they won't give me mine."

I try to reassure him that he will receive his breakfast.

Early that evening, I receive another call.

"Hi, this is Mark from Sunshine Villa. Your dad has been gone since breakfast."

I look out the window. Rose colored clouds stand out in relief to the charcoal gray-blue of the sky. Soon, it will be night. I think about the bumper sticker on cars: "Do you know where your child is?"

Mark continues. "We've notified the police. Do you know that he's been hitchhiking?"

"Dad said he met a man on the wharf who drove him somewhere. He asked me for a ride to his house so he could thank him, but he only had a partial address. I think that was the only time."

"He's been hitchhiking quite a bit. We've been trying to keep an eye on him, but he's a determined man. Anyway, I wanted to tell you that he's missing. You might hear from him."

"Thanks, Mark. I'll let you know if he shows up and of course you'll call me immediately."

Although Sunshine Villa sits above Beach Flats and the Boardwalk, both dangerous for my dad, I reassure myself that he would not be drawn to either place. He's probably downtown or hitchhiking a ride to Wal-Mart. I hope whoever picks him up is a kind person. Dad has always been surrounded by good karma. When I'm in the car with him, we find a parking place right in front of wherever we're going. I tell myself again and again that he's ok. At dinner time, I'm not hungry.

At 9:00 that night the phone rings and I rush to pick it up. "Hi this is Joan at Sunshine Villa. Your dad is back safe and sound."

"What happened?"

"Mary who works here was off duty and ran into your dad at Long's drugstore. She gave him a ride back."

"What was he doing?"

"I think he had just finished eating somewhere."

"I'm happy he's safe. Sorry he caused you so much trouble."

I immediately call Dad in his room. "I was worried about you. I heard you had quite an adventure today."

His voice fills with pride. "The head of driving in the state of California granted me a special driver's license."

"Oh yeah? How did you get there?"

"I took the bus. I spent almost all day there taking the test and talking to different people. I met the guy who runs the place. He is the head of all licenses given in the state of Indiana, I mean California, you know where I am. I have a driver's license now."

I wonder if they told him that at the DMV so he would finally leave. "Dad, I'm happy you're safe."

The next morning I'm roused from sleep at 4:00 am. He screams into the telephone: "You stole my driver's license and wallet." He has also lost his hearing aid and a pair of glasses. David and I are packed to go camping, but I can't leave Dad in this condition. I go to Sunshine Villa and help locate his glasses and give him some money. I alert the staff to keep an eye out for his wallet. We stay around that day to ensure that he will be okay and leave a day later for our camping trip.

This is a different kind of camping adventure for David and me. We usually go backpacking, but this time have decided to take our mountain bikes, our dog, Liat and car camp. I'm relieved that we won't be somewhere in the back country of the Sierras away from a phone, and I'll be able to retrieve my messages from the answering machine, if something drastic happens with Dad.

I've been wanting to hang out near a lake where it's warm and I can swim, so we've planned to camp at Clear Lake in northern California. Bill has warned me that a forest fire is raging in the area, but David believes that reality is as he wants it to be. Because we plan to camp there, he says the fire isn't that bad. As we approach Clear Lake, my eyes begin to burn.

"How're you doin?" I ask him, wondering how long his denial will last.

"Pretty good," he answers

I sneeze. "The air or lack of it is getting to me. It looks gray over to the right where the lake is."

"Do you think it's going to rain?"

I look at him with disbelief. "It's the fire."

"What do you want to do?"

"Let's pull into that gas station and find out what's going on."

I open the van door and Liat quickly jumps out and rushes over to some dry looking bushes, smells them and squats. She trots back to me, her tail held high and proud, brushes my leg and then begins wandering around, her nose close to the ground. I walk into the office with David following behind.

While uncertainty causes me to speed up, it slows David down. He clears his throat. "About the lake." He pauses and clears his throat again. "it's over there to the east. I was wondering if there's camping there?"

"Sure."

43

My patience quota is used up. "How close to the lake is the fire and are the camp grounds open?"

"They may be open, but I wouldn't stay there. Fire's burning badly and smoke is everywhere. Can't you smell it?"

David asks: "Where would you suggest we camp?"

"Here's a map of recreation areas in California and Oregon." He opens it on the glass counter in front of David. I can't see over the two of them, so I walk to the van to get Liat's bowl and fill it with water. While she's slurping up a drink, David comes over to me with the map. "The guy says that here, by the Klamath River in Oregon is a good spot." He outlines a route with his finger.

"How long will it take us to get there?"

"A couple of hours. What do you think?"

"Sounds good to me."

That night I call on the pay phone and check my answering machine. No messages from Sunshine Villa about Dad. The next morning the sun light finds it way through the tall redwood branches. It's a nice break from the Santa Cruz summer fog. David, Liat and I run on a dirt path which weaves through the campground. After a half a mile it opens up to a road which plays tag with the Klamath river. We follow another trail until we arrive at a wide portion of the river. Tall granite rocks border it on one side and on the other is a sandy beach. Clear water flows over its rock bottom. When the day warms, it will be a great place to swim.

We return to the campground where Liat makes a bed for herself in the dirt, falls asleep, and begins snoring. Unsure of how much territory she was supposed to guard, she spent most of the night running around chasing things. She briefly raises her head when we tie her to a tree and then resumes sleeping. Leaving her with water and food, David and I set out on our mountain bikes. The route winds uphill through tall redwoods and resembles many of the bicycle rides in the Santa Cruz mountains. Thankfully, no logging trucks ask us to share the road, and we even bike through a tree with a hole in it.

On our return, Liat leaps up and down with excitement. We put on our bathing suits and head for the river. Young boys are jumping and diving off the rocks into the water. I jump off a rock too. Liat stands on it barking as if to say, "Don't leave me. Come right back."

"Here Liat," I coax her. She runs back and forth barking until finally mustering her courage, jumps into the water after me. We swim to the other side. David is sitting on the ground and I throw myself down beside him. Liat shakes water all over us.

I place an arm around David's back and tell him, "Thank you so much for coming here. I think I'm in heaven."

"You haven't mentioned your dad once."

"I've thought about him but don't feel so worried. It's great to have this peaceful time."

Driving home we follow the coast from Mendocino and don't turn inland until San Francisco. A couple of times the white sand and cool breezes beckon us to stop, walk the beaches and wade and splash in the water. Generally, though we are content to watch the scenery slide by the window, not breaking the silence with talk or music from the car tape deck.

At the house David empties the car, Liat smells every rose bush and tree, while I bring in the stack of mail, and listen to the messages on the answering machine. As I remove the clothing from the back pack, I smell each item, inhaling wood smoke, cedar, redwood and wild rosemary. My clothes don't ever smell of body odor when I'm camping, but they are usually covered with dirt and soot. I'm sorry they need to be washed. We retire early that night looking forward to sleeping in a bed rather than the ground. Neither of us feel like talking, as our legs caressing is enough conversation.

The next morning on entering my waiting room, I notice that the light is flashing on the answering machine. It's a message from he director of the Sunshine Village asking me to call back at my convenience. Sometimes when calling Sunshine Village I'm put on a hold for quite a while, but this time I'm connected quickly. She begins with, "Hello, I'm sorry, but I don't think this is the best place for your father. He's too much for us to handle and needs a locked facility."

My throat is tight, so the words sputter out. "Where can he go next?"

"You might want to try The Mansion." Her voice is kinds as she adds, "we like your dad and are sorry it isn't working out."

"How long before I need to find another place?"

"How about a couple of weeks." She adds again: "Try the Mansion".

I call the Senior Center. They give me a list of places, and they too mention The Mansion.

Next I call David at work. He's a busy with a patient and will call me back. I don't have a client until 11:00. I try to go over some of my charts, checking the billing and any other paper work I may have missed. The phone rings at 10:30. It's David.

"Hello." His calm slow voice is a relief.

"Dad has to leave Sunshine Villa."

"Why?"

"I guess they feel that they can't handle him. He's too much for them."

"Let me talk to them."

"What are you going to say?"

"Maybe I can work something out. They should be able to figure this out."

I hang up the phone and stare at a picture of a wolf that a client gave me. I say to the wolf: "Dad is too much for anyone to handle except Mom." The way she dug in, even my father succumbed to her. I don't think Sunshine Villa or anyone else, except me, has that kind of investment in my dad.

Later in the day as I'm finishing my lunch, the phone rings. "Hello, David here." he begins in his doctor voice.

"Hello," I answer back. "Helen here, remember, your wife."

"Sure, I'm sorry. I know who you are."

"Of course, you do. You called me."

"I talked with Sunshine Villa. They like your dad, think he's charming and adorable but don't want to take responsibility for his safety."

"I know, David. I understand. Thanks for trying." I took care of David's father when he had cancer. He died in our house and now David wants to do his part. But I know that nothing more can be done.

That night our love making is fierce. It reminds me of the night when David's father died. I want him to enter me deeply, to fill me with life so that it rises up and down and through me. I grab his shoulders tightly. Hips rub and abrade hips, lips reach and suck. We push and meld together. I let go with a sob as life heaves against and within me. I sleep well that night, grateful for David's soft breaths and occasional snores beside me.

PART 6
THE MANSION

I decide to follow the recommendation of Sunshine Villa and set up an appointment with DeeDee, the owner of The Mansion. The facility is 5 miles up a country road. I make a sharp left hand turn and am immediately stopped at a spiked gate. A black iron fence with rails shaped like pointed spears surrounds the property. Beyond the gate is a long driveway. Flowers cover the front porch. Like Sunshine Villa it sits on top of a hill. No one can enter or leave the property without pushing a button and being admitted by someone inside the house who opens the gate.

To call the place a mansion is pretentious. The building is a sprawling country house on top of a grassy knoll. It's dark inside. Antique dishes and artifacts are protected in cases. The population is small, maybe 14 to 20 residents. The dining room is cozy and meals are served family style.

Unlike Sunshine Villa, the rooms are unfurnished. That will be okay because Dusty is driving across country with a truck full of items from the house in Marion.

Dee Dee suggests that I take my dad to visit some of the other locked facilities in Santa Cruz. After that, The Mansion might be more appealing to him. She also tells me that for Dad to be placed in a locked facility, I need a Conservatorship, a legal document that says that he is incompetent and unable to make decisions for himself. She advises me to take care of that as soon as possible.

I acquire a list of locked facilities from the Senior Center and set off with my dad to visit them. The first place is managed by a sweet Hispanic couple. They have a little girl about 18-months-old. My father is delighted with her. The facility is functional, no frilly curtains or antiques which is fine with my father. He won't be able to have his own room, though. I see this as a problem and have visions of him physically threatening his roommate who he accuses of stealing his things. The other problem is that the residents are prevented from wandering by means of a wrist bracelet which triggers an alarm whenever one of them passes a certain point on the grounds. I can imagine yelling fights as efforts are made to stop my dad from leaving.

The next facility we visit is devoid of any furniture and decorations. The residents sleep in beds lined up against the wall, divided by thin curtains. The men appear as one gray blur, almost indistinguishable from

47

the curtains and the bed. They hardly move, seem to be heavily medicated and inhabit an autistic world barely recognizing our presence. One resident, a woman in her sixties, latches on to Dad and me.

"Look at my tennis shoes," she says grabbing Dad's hand and tap dancing in front of him. "Who are you? My name is Daisy. Are you going to live here with me? I live here. What's your name?" She talks non stop and reminds me of a loquacious three-year-old. Mrs. Rogers, manger of the facility has given her the tennis shoes as a present and Daisy can't seem to stop dancing in them. I'm reminded of the story: "The Red Shoes". The little girl wants the shoes, but once they are on her feet, she can't stop dancing, no matter how tired and desperate she feels. Daisy seems to be stricken with the same kind of frantic energy. She is a frenzy of colorful movement against the gray chorus of the men.

Although Mrs. Rogers appears to me as a strong, kind woman, the thought of Dad living in such a place horrifies me. Daisy tries to follow Dad and me out the door. Dad gently takes her arm and brings her back to Mrs. Rogers.

The third and last place we visit is the Mansion; and of course, he likes it the best. Dad will have his own room. The back door opens into a large field. Residents are walking around and talking with one another. When it's time to leave and return to Sunshine Villa, he says: "Do we have to go? I want to stay here now."

The two women attendants, Jo and Linda smile and pat him on the arm. They reassure him that they will see him soon.

The next day DeeDee hands me twelve pages of documents I need to fill out before my father can move into The Mansion. She says begrudgingly: "He has more rights now than you and I put together."

I think to myself: "He needs these protections. He's disabled and confused about reality and no one will believe him because he fabricates or misunderstands so much. She also shows me a book called <u>Validation, The Feil Method</u> by Naomi Feil and explains that the author's premise is one shouldn't argue with the disoriented elderly, but instead accept their reality. I certainly feel that I have been too attached to my own reality with Dad and decide to buy a copy. DeeDee gives me a list of items Dad will need--four pairs of pants, eight shirts, eight pairs of underpants, etc. Billy drives down from Berkeley and we meet at Sunshine Villa to pack Dad for his move. I purchase laundry pens to mark his clothes.

Even though Bill is frustrated and hurt by Dad's refusal to give him the power of attorney, he is calm and patient with him. I give Bill a marking pen and I have one for myself. As Dee Dee instructed, we begin writing his name in all of his clothing. Once more, I'm struck by how much this reminds me of sending a child to camp. Dad seems content to be in our presence and allows us to begin organizing his possessions. He is much happier about this move than when he left his house in Marion. He walks around us chatting, picking up items, examining them and putting them down again.

The surprise begins when we open his drawers. I knew that he had a stash of bananas, but he has also taken ten sets of place servings from the dining room. Dinner rolls, crackers, packages of cheese are in the refrigerator and wrapped up neatly in napkins in ornamental arrangements around lamps and in the bathroom. Dad has been accusing others of stealing his possessions, but he has been doing a good job hoarding some of theirs.

To my horror I also discover envelopes and bank statements. I've been trying to accumulate and list all of his accounts both for tax purposes and to prepare an accounting for the Conservatorship. Using copies of the power of attorney, I have rerouted his mail from Marion, Indiana to my house. Simultaneously, he has been rerouting it back to his address at Sunshine Villa.

Bill and I wrap up the silverware in a towel and take it to the front desk. Linda is there. She, like many of the people that staff the front desk, is young, attractive and patient. "We're returning these from Dad's room. The dining staff might need them." I open the towel and Billy counts out almost ten complete sets of knives, forks and spoons.

"Don't you think I need a receipt?" Dad asks.

Billy jokes, "Maybe you should be giving them a receipt for taking them."

"No. They need to give me a written receipt." His voice is becoming demanding.

I decide to distract him. "Let's go out and have a really nice dinner on the wharf. Doesn't that sound good Dad?" He decides to give up the silverware.

Riva's Fish House is a moderately priced restaurant with good food, fast service; and the tables are placed by windows, with a view of the beach and boardwalk on one side; and on the other, a view of the beach in front of the Dream Inn. Dad is happy with his salmon and I remind him that this is the place where we bought the great gelato a couple of weeks ago. During dinner, he doesn't say much, seems content to listen to Bill and me talk. He is more relaxed than he has been in a long time.

After dinner Bill drives me back to my car at Sunshine Villa. I take off knowing that I will never return here again. Dad stays with Bill and he follows me to The Mansion. I press the button and the voice at the intercom says they are expecting us. The gate slides open and both cars enter. The sun is still shining and the air is warm. They have provided furnishings on loan until Dad's things arrive on the truck from Indiana with Dusty. In the meantime he has developed a fixation with canned mandarin oranges, demanding large quantities. Dee Dee suggests I buy a couple of boxes on sale to help with his transition. I deliver these quietly to the kitchen, and Bill and I drive to our separate homes.

A week later Dusty arrives with Dad's furniture. I'm sorting through boxes of photographs and letters he has retrieved from the house in Marion. I've decided to make a photograph album for Dad, which I call: "A Book of Memories". I'm also reading the letters. Dad saved the family's correspondence. He has love letters between Mom and him, letters that my brothers and I wrote to each other as well as to Mom and Dad. He has even saved the correspondence between his siblings and his mother. I'm reading a letter Dad wrote to his younger brother, Dan while Dad was in college. Dan developed cancer ten years ago and wanted to sit down with Dad and separate their assets. Dad became paranoid and accused him of not being fair. This was the incipient stages of my dad's Alzheimers and no one was certain what was happening. Dad was continually trying to find the right papers that would prove his point. This carried on for a year until Dan finally sued my dad for closure. Their disagreement caused a rift in the family, and Jim, Dan's eldest son, and Bill stopped speaking. I loved Uncle Dan. When I was first married, he and I sent each other our poetry for review and commentary. I was the only one who went to Indiana to say goodby to Uncle Dan before he died. In the letter Dad is accusing Dan of having stolen his pajamas.

I put it down and reach in the box and pull out a picture of my mother lying on the ground in a bathing suit and smiling. I remember asking Dad about that picture. He said it was taken the day he asked her to marry him. The door bell rings. I put the picture back in the box and open the door. Standing there is my step-son, Aaron. His brown hair is cut short and jelled to spike up. His lips are soft and smiling and I melt into his big bear hug. He is married and lives in San Jose with his wife Siobhan. "What are you doing here? I'm happy to see you but am surprised."

"I know you've been having a hard time with your dad so I thought I would stop by and see how you're doing."

Myrrhia must have heard his voice and runs from her bedroom and folds herself into his arms. "Aaron." Liat starts to bark.

In a stern voice I say to Liat: "Okay, that's enough." I turn back to Aaron, "Are you hungry or thirsty? Where's Siobhan?"

"She's studying. What have you here?"

"They're photos Dusty brought from the house in Marion. I'm putting selected pictures in an album for Dad and am calling it his 'Book of Memories'." I hand him a photograph. It was taken on the day I married

50

his father. Aaron was seven years old. My dad is kneeling down and talking and Aaron is looking intensely into his face. "I've always wondered about this picture."

He studies it. "I remember. Your dad said to me if I ever needed anything to let him know and that he would always be there to help." He hands the picture back.

My eyes tear and Myrrhia hugs me. "Why are you crying? Do you miss your Dad?"

I guess, Myrrhia. I miss him but am so happy to have you and Aaron. Maybe I'm getting my period. I don't know."

"It's okay Mommy. Aaron and I love you. We'll be here to help you."

Dad hates being locked in. DeeDee has given me the name of a woman, Sarah, who comes and takes him out a couple times of week. He also thoroughly enjoys "Cindi's Celebrations". Cindi drives around in a large van and picks up the elderly in assisted living facilities and their own homes. Sometimes, she takes them to a restaurant and at other times she has luncheons in her own home. Dad likes any opportunity to leave the Mansion. While there, he creates as much hassle for the staff as he did at Sunshine Villa. Many of the residents are older women and he takes it upon himself to rescue them. He introduces me to one of the residents, Gladys. She carries a large purse and seems quite self-assured.

"I'm a doctor," she tells me. "I've known your father for a long time. We went to college together and served on several hospital committees. We are old friends."

I look at Dad. He raises his eyebrows and give me a look that says ... go along with it.

"What's in your purse?" I ask her. She opens it up and there is a large alarm clock and a mirror.

Jo calls me over to the station. "I need to talk to you a minute. We had to unplug your dad's phone. It will only be for awhile."

"Why?"

"One of our new residents..."

"You mean Gladys?"

"No, there's another new resident. See over there. Her name is Louise. Well she's convinced that her car was stolen and your dad has been calling 911 to help her out."

"Did they come?"

"No, but it seems better to allow some time for things to quiet for awhile."

51

We go to Erik's Deli where he loudly orders his usual corned beef sandwich with no fat and a Caesar salad with no croutons. As always, he is reassured that the beef will be lean or they will suggest something else.

We are seated at a table waiting for our food. My dad is upset and aggressive, and I'm happy that there is no one in there I know. "You don't know what goes on there at that place, that house," he says. "They're all smiles to you, but that isn't how they are really."

"You mean The Mansion. What do they do?"

"You know," he says. "You're pretending not to know. They take your things. I'm locked in here like a puppy and you pull my chain."

Our lunches arrive and I decide to change the subject. I talk to him about Myrrhia. "You know it looks like she will be valedictorian when she graduates this year."

"Well, that's something," he says. "Does she know where she wants to go to college?"

"She likes art, math and writing. I'm not sure."

"The art is just something to play with. Of course, she won't study art."

Now I'm on familiar territory with my dad. I could argue with him about the value of art, but I'm tired of fighting.

"She should go to Harvard," he says.

"She doesn't want to go."

"That's a parent's job, to guide their children. She doesn't know what she needs."

Good luck guiding Myrrhia, I think to myself. Here he is telling me I should control Myrrhia, this man who hates to be controlled himself. "We'll see about it," I say. We finish our meal in silence.

Chapter 7
The Skateboard Accident

Myrrhia asks me to take her to the chiropractor in Los Gatos. She says her knee hurts from the time she crashed on her skateboard.

"I can't drive you to Los Gatos right now. I have too much going on with Dad here. How about you drive yourself or see Dr. Kim, the chiropractor in Santa Cruz?"

"I'll be okay."

The next day one of her friends, Sachem comes to the door and knocks. His normally pink cheeks are white. I start to tell him that Myrrhia isn't home when I see her limping up the walk. The skin of one leg is torn and bleeding and her knee is swollen.

Sachem speaks softly: "There was an accident. His eyes are only partly open and his mouth is tight and pinched.

"What happened?"

"She was skating Laurel Street hill."

Myrrhia reaches my arms, lets out a gasp and then begins to sob. I hold her for awhile and listen to the sounds of the pain she has been holding and saving for me. I know it is my job as her parent to tolerate her pain, but I can barely stand it.

While we're standing there, David comes home.

"There's been an accident," I tell him, my voice sounding calmer than I feel.

He responds in a flat tight voice, "I know, Myrrhia called me on my cell phone. Let me take a look at her."

As I watch him examine her legs and hands, for the first time I notice how much skin is missing from them. "She'll need skin grafts and knee surgery," he states angrily, betraying his underlying fear. "Now you've done it. You'll have to let me wash the debris and disinfect it."

I remember Dad cleaning my leg after I had jumped from David Ganz's go-kart. He gently tried to remove the small pebbles and dirt out of the cuts, but it hurt like hell. He and Mom's best friend, Mrs. Jones gave me scotch to cut the pain. To this day I hate the taste of scotch. But how is David to clean her wounds which cover most of her leg? I go into the kitchen for some brandy.

I hear Myrrhia screaming from the bathroom, then David's exasperated voice: "This isn't working. You have to be quiet."

"Can't I just get in the bathtub and soak it off?"

I come into the bathroom. "That's a good idea. Here, you adjust the water temperature and drink this brandy. It will help. Drink as much of it as you can and wash this down with it." I hand her an advil.

"I might need to scream, Dad."

David's voice is hard and his lips are so thin and tight that they almost disappear. He says, "I'm leaving for awhile. Put ice on her knee."

"Okay." I hear the front door slam. Myrrhia sobs. I can hardly stand this.

"Mom, I can't put my entire leg in the water. It hurts."

"All you can do is try honey."

"Leave the room and shut the door. You don't want to be in here now."

I hear loud screams from the bathroom. I start to cry but stop myself. I can't afford to break down into self pity. I tell myself Dad is fine at The Mansion. Myrrhia is young and will heal, it's all okay. Soon she limps from the bathroom. I place her on the couch with an ice pack for her knee and carefully hand her a bowl of hot soup.

The next day David takes Myrrhia to his office to x-ray her knee and check out her wounds. What a kid, her skin is already healing. She'll need to be on crutches for awhile but her knee isn't as badly injured as he thought. However, she can't skate board the three miles to school anymore, and I don't see how I can make time in my schedule to pick her up. Blair suggests I have her take a taxi home from school. Now I have two family members being shuttled on lift lines and taxis.

Chapter 8
The Conservatorship

A Conservatorship will grant me the authority to handle Dad's possessions, money, and place him in a locked facility. Unlike the Power of Attorney, he will not be able to undo this document. As Dad is contesting this Conservatorship, I need to go to court and prove that he is unable to care for himself. Although it is obvious that his brain isn't operating on all of it's cylinders, the idea that I will have my father declared mentally incompetent in court is appalling.

I'm riding a stationary bike at the gym, when the man next to me begins a conversation. He's good looking, with silver curly hair. "How're you doing?" he asks. "You used to come here regularly, but I haven't seen you for awhile."

"I've been busy. My dad has Alzheimers and he's been taking up a lot of my time."

"You still need to work out."

"I'm running in the mornings; and believe me, I miss being here. But I have to declare my father mentally incompetent to keep him in a locked facility. I see homeless people talking to themselves, and they don't have to be locked up."

I 'm surprised that I have revealed so much to him.

"You need to look at it this way," he says. "Your dad isn't wandering the streets because he has family. Those people out there have no one who cares about them.

You're looking out for your dad."

I smile at him "Thank you. When you put it that way, it seems so simple."

But it isn't all that simple. First, I need to find a lawyer who agrees to handle the Conservatorship. I start with references from friends. Several lawyers I call do not want to, as they put it, "take on a contested Conservatorship". Finally, one agrees, Nick Wyckoff. We arrange a meeting at his office on Water Street. It is a one story building built with bricks painted beige. I must have driven by a hundred times and never noticed it. The receptionist has brown hair with silver threads. She's wearing a rose colored suit. The skirt is, in between straight and a-line, and a beige lacy polyester blouse is visible underneath the matching jacket. "I'm here about my father," I tell her.

"I know." She smiles and says that Nick is expecting me. "This Alzheimers business is so hard on families. Follow me." Her friendly direct manner reminds me of the women who worked at my dad's store.

She escorts me to another office at the back. It is a room with a large brown table surrounded by walls lined by books. The table, the floor and the books are all brown. Mr. Wyckoff enters the room and extends his hand. "Hello, I'm Nick Wyckoff. You can call me Nick." He had sandy blond hair, blue eyes, fair skin and is average height. His face is kind and friendly.

He explains to me the process of the Conservatorship. Because Dad is contesting it, we will need to go to court. If the judge thinks Dad should be conserved, a date will be set. It marks the beginning of the Conservatorship and the total of all of his assets must be calculated from that date. This makes things difficult. I point out that date is in the middle of the month and the bank statements are dated at the end. "Does that mean I need to calculate a percentage for the amount for that month?"

"Look," he says. "This is too complicated. You will need an accountant."

"But isn't it a simple algebraic equation?"

"This is one of the most difficult Conservatorships I have ever seen. Your dad has endless accounts. You need a professional."

"Do you have any suggestions?"

"You will have to take care of that."

"That means I'll need two accountants, one for Dad's taxes in Indiana and one for the Conservatorship here."

"I guess so."

I like numbers. While in graduate school, I enjoyed the aspect of my research that involved data analysis and was a teaching assistant for undergraduate statistics. Numbers have no hidden emotional agendas. They don't have hurt feelings or need to manipulate or control. They are always dependable and reliable; and so far, they have been the only predictable part of this Conservatorship. However, it will be nice to have an accountant handle this and relieve me of one more task.

The days begin for me at 5:00 am., that is when I am not awakened by Dad screaming into the phone at 2:00 am. I quietly leave my bed and am followed by the parade of the dog and cat marching behind me to the kitchen. The cat meows loudly for her food. The dog follows cheerfully knowing that she will be allowed to lick the empty cat food can. I make decaf coffee, turn on the computer, and sign on line to check my e-mail. Since I brought Dad out from Indiana, Aaron has been sending me great jokes. I imagine him in his cubicle at work corresponding with his friends in similar gray boxes scattered about San Jose.

After reading the jokes, I begin listing every financial record of Dad's I can find. I'm trying to close these accounts and transfer the funds to a bank in Santa Cruz, which will eventually become his Conservatorship account. I also need to have a record of every cent I receive and any money I spend. He has quite a few bills to pay for instance, his rent at Sunshine Villa and now the Mansion, doctor visits, clothes, food expenses, not to mention the unpaid bills from Marion that continually pop up. Meanwhile, Dad is calling the banks trying to keep his accounts open. This causes the people I talk with to be suspicious of me. They have their own special documents they want me to complete and have notarized. To make difficult matters worse, Dad has been calling his lawyer to undo the power of attorney.

The morning of the court hearing I set an alarm and begin dressing. It is black outside with no moon to brighten the day. We need to be in court at 8:00. As Dad is slow, I plan to arrive at the Mansion by 5:30 am to dress him. As I head up the road into the Santa Cruz mountains, I wish that one of my brothers was here to help me. Neither have expressed any concern about this process, which surprises me. I wonder if they know how anxious I am. Maybe it wouldn't bother either of them to take Dad to court. Bill is a lawyer and familiar with court rooms. He hasn't asked if I need help or even how I'm feeling. Dusty seems to have forgotten about Dad for awhile and has found it difficult to make a commitment for a time to come visit. Bill has been more consistent coming every other week to take Dad out to dinner. The crazy thing is that Dad doesn't even remember the visits. Bill drives down from Berkeley, hangs out with him, takes him out and then the next day Dad calls and complains that he hasn't seen Bill or Dusty and asks when are they coming. Even when I give Dad the name of the restaurant where Bill says he has taken him, Dad denies it's ever happened. Then, he wants again to know when Bill is coming. I tell him a day and that calms him. He asks about Dusty; and I say, some day.

"Why?" he asks. "Why can't Dusty say when he will be here?"

"I don't know Dad. He doesn't like to commit himself more than an hour or a two at a time."

"But can't he just give me a day?"

"I guess not."

David offers to go to court with me, but as Dad is already accusing him of stealing his things, I don't think it is a good idea to involve him. My friend Rebecca Nolan suggests that she accompany me, but her back gives out, and she is flat on the floor. Then, Rebecca Campbell offers to assist but at the last minute has to cancel. Her nephew is a Canadian citizen, and she has a meeting with a lawyer so he can continue to stay and work at her business.   Instead, she invites us to her bakery for breakfast before the hearing.

When I drive the hill up to the Mansion, the sky although dark is clear allowing the stars to shine through the breaks in the trees, and the air has an autumn chill. I speak into the intercom at the gate, announcing my name. A voice answers, and the gate slides open. The house looks dark. I find Dad's room and knock on the door. Although it is respectful behavior to knock before entering a room, he is hard of hearing and the knock is never functional. I push the door open. One of the staff members has already awakened him and laid out his suit.

I help him dress. Buttoning his shirts, zipping his pants and threading the belt through the loops are especially difficult tasks for him. I hold out his blue jacket with the Kiwanis pin. He asks, "Do I look nice?"

"Yes, you look very dignified."

He is excited by this process. "Are we going to court now?"

"First I thought we'd stop at Rebecca's bakery and have breakfast. You remember Rebecca don't you?"

"Of course."

The sky is beginning to lighten as we enter "Rebecca's Mighty Muffins". Bless her heart, she is waiting there for us. She puts an arm around him and flashes a smile. Rebecca is beautiful. She is tall, with golden brown curly hair, blue eyes and moves with grace and elegance. Dad is attracted to her and stands a little taller. His eyes brighten and a smile softens his face.

"What would you like for breakfast?" she asks. She takes his hand and walks with him over to the case full of muffins. "What do you like?"

"Let's see, I like blueberries."

"One of these?" she asks him. She reaches into the case and places a fat muffin bursting with blueberries on a plate. "Should I heat it for you?"

"That would be nice."

"How about some fresh orange juice?"

"Orange juice too, great."

She reaches in the refrigerator and takes out a small bottle of Odwalla orange juice and walks with the muffin to a table. Dad and I follow and we sit together.

"This muffin is good," Dad says.

"You and Helen are going to court today."

"Yes. We need to settle this business, so I can finish my work, file these papers. How do I look?"

"Wonderful," Rebecca says and gives him a big hug and smile.

Dad and I leave the bakery. "This is a beautiful morning," he says. It's a Santa Cruz September morning and the fog has begun to obscure the sun so that it appears as a vague orange ball trying to find its way through the clouds. I'm not so certain about it being such a great day, but seeing my Dad happy helps me relax a little.

We drive to the county building. The fog becomes heavier and a mist forms on the windshield, so I turn on the wipers. Dad begins saying "tap, tap, tap" in time with the blades. I try not to be irritated but I'm wound up about court. For Dad, court is different. He finally has his day. He wasn't able to sue the phone company, the plumbing and heating companies, his automobile insurance carrier, but now he can have his chance to argue with me.

Nick, the lawyer for the Conservatorship is waiting for us. I introduce Dad to him. Dad thinks Nick is his lawyer. "Hello, my name is Bill Resneck, Helen's father. I'm so happy to see you. We're counting on you to straighten this mess out and return my accounts to me." I decide not to correct him. The truth would only make him angry and doesn't seem to matter so much anymore. The court room is fluorescent light bright. Dad looks to me for what to do next and I find seats for us. I, like Dad have dressed well for this occasion, wearing a dress and a scarf. My hair is clean and I feel professional. Dad stands tall and his thin gray hair is brushed back. With his navy sport coat, he looks handsome, a man who knows how to handle himself and people. Yet, I know that I am the one in charge, his guide.

One at a time, lawyers are called before the judge. Most of them the judge reprimands for not following certain points of order or tells them that they need more information about various legal items. I wonder if Nick will be scolded. "What is happening?" Dad asks. He isn't whispering. As he always says: "I'm deaf in one ear and can't hear out of the other."

His good ear is next to mine and I try to whisper. "These lawyers are presenting different cases."

"The judge is mad at them."

"Well, I don't know about that."

Our name is called. Dad says he does not want a Conservatorship. The judge appoints him his own attorney, Tim Volkman. Although Tim has the appropriate courtroom dress of conservative suit, tie, and shiny leather shoes, he is obviously young and has an innocent boyish look. I can't imagine that this is a job he wants, to defend a demented proud old man, but the judge has appointed him, so he accepts. He introduces himself to Dad, but Dad still thinks Nick is his attorney. Before Dad and I leave, Nick, Tim, and I set up an appointment. Dad shakes Nick's hand and thanks him again for his help.

Nick and I meet with Tim at his office downtown. I take an elevator up to the second floor where Nick and Tim wait for me in a narrow room with a long wooden table. He offers us coffee and then asks to see copies of the documents and papers I have. I give him a copy of the power of attorney. He hands it to his secretary who makes a copy. "Is there anything else I should know?" he asks.

Nick answers, "He's been staying at Sunshine Villa and The Mansion and you say Dr. Gillette has evaluated him?"

"That's right," I answer. "He was also evaluated by a psychiatrist in Indianapolis."

"I don't think I will need that. Anything else?" Tim asks.

"That's all we have," Nick answers.

"We'll see you in court then," Tim reaches out his hand.

"One more thing," I tell them. "Don't embarrass him. He's my dad."

Nick looks at Tim and Tim answers. "My grandmother and grandfather both have Alzheimers. I understand what you're going through. We'll try to be as considerate as possible."

"Thanks. It's been a pleasure." I shake both of their hands and leave the room. I take the elevator down by myself. I guess they have some other things to discuss.

The end of October, a month later, I drive up to The Mansion for the next court appearance. The sky seems even darker than it had the month before. Dad's clothes aren't laid out for him. He hasn't washed in awhile and needs a shave. I look in his closet for a coat but he refuses to wear one. I think to myself, "This is trouble. I don't want to do this."

I pull out the blue sport coat. "Don't you want to wear this with your Kiwanis pin?"

"Don't try to fool me with that pin."

I take out the beige one. "How about this?"

"What are you doing Helen? You're trying to confuse me."

I say to myself: What's a sport coat anyway? It really isn't necessary.

Again, we drive down to Mighty Muffins to have breakfast with Rebecca. I give her a big long hug, feel good having her hold me.

She says, "I know it's hard honey. You look nice, a little thin with all of the stress, but that's a pretty dress,"

"I'm not dressed up," Dad yells. "I need a sport coat. Why did you allow me to come like this?"

I try to calm him down. "It doesn't matter Dad. You look fine."

Rebecca adds laughing, "You look great."

"No I don't," he asserts. "Call The Mansion. They'll bring me a coat."

"I can't do that Dad." It's a 20 minute drive from The Mansion and the staff already feels he's a strain, but I know that's not a concept he can grasp. "Let's eat breakfast. Don't you want a muffin or some juice? Let's look at the counter."

"Who eats all of this food?" he asks

"Well, you can eat some of it. Do you want to try a blueberry again?"

"You like blueberry," says Rebecca, remembering his choice from the last time. While he slowly eats a muffin, he becomes lost in the muffin wrapper, turning it over and folding it and refolding it. The Alzheimers genie who lives behind my father's eyes has taken away the liveliness and intelligence. They are vacant. Once when Myrrhia was two or three-years-old I hired a teenage girl to watch her while David and I went out to dinner for a couple of hours. The girl was very nice, but a little slow intellectually. When I asked Myrrhia how it went, she said: "Mommy, it didn't go well. That girl was a vacant lot." That's what my dad's eyes look like now, a vacant lot.

Dad slowly eats his muffin and sips his juice. He begins folding the muffin paper again and I tell him: "It's time to go. Thanks for everything Rebecca."

Dad says emphatically, "I'm not going like this. Call The Mansion." Some feeling is back in his eyes, but they are hard and he isn't fully present.

"Let's go to court and see what your lawyer thinks. If he says you need a coat, we'll drive back up there and get you one."

The gray court building matches the gray sky. I hope this works out. I don't know what they will do if Dad throws a tantrum. I worry that they will put him in jail or the psychiatric ward, or God forbid, have to schedule the damn hearing again.

Nick and Tom are waiting outside the courtroom. I say to each of them, "Dad is worried about how he's dressed. Does he need a jacket?"

Nick reassures him. "You look fine Mr. Resneck. After all, this is Santa Cruz, you know California. People don't dress up so much here. It's not like Indiana."

Tim agrees, "You look fine."

"I wanted to look nice but Helen wouldn't take me back to get my coat. Once this is settled, I can do these things for myself. It's frustrating."

We enter the courtroom and I find Dad a kleenex. His nose has been dripping and I think he has developed allergies in Santa Cruz. We sit down and Dad holds my hand. The same woman who was present at the last hearing is sitting by the judge and taking notes. I'm not certain of her role, but she has a kind face and smiles at me. I think I should return her smile but I'm not certain that I feel like smiling right now. Then I remember a day long ago when I was about four or five-years old and I'm walking with Billy

61

and Dad. It's a bright sunny day and I think we are downtown in Marion. A woman stops and talks to us and gives me an apple. She doesn't offer Billy or Dad anything and I ask my dad about that. "She liked your smile. When you smile, you can have anything Helen. Remember to always smile." I don't like the idea of being forced to smile; and if pressured to perform, will dig in my heels and not budge. However, this time I realize I'm grateful for the smile. It has been a difficult morning with Dad, and I think maybe she sees something sweet between us. I smile back at her.

This is a trial and the various people who have been involved in Dad's life in Santa Cruz must testify. John Gillette, the psychiatrist reports on his stay at Sunshine Villa, how he roamed Santa Cruz and the police were required to return him. He also brings up the incident at The Mansion last week in which Dad reached out to stab one of the staff with a fork. I want to protest. The guy grabbed his bowl from him when he wasn't ready to give it up. Don't you understand Alzheimers? It's like dealing with two year olds. He would have given up the bowl in his own time. And so what if he didn't? So what if he took it back to his room? You could have retrieved the bowl later, when he'd forgotten about it. But I'm worried. What if Dad really is crazy, had suddenly stabbed him without good provocation? But he should have asked Dad if he was finished. He wouldn't have stabbed him for no reason. I say nothing. It's to my benefit if they hear this story as is.

Dr. Gillette continues his testimony. He says: "Helen has tried to be fair with her father and give him as much independence as he can manage, but I certainly believe that he needs to be in a locked facility. Mr. Resneck, although in his eighties, is a vigorous man. He's had many escapades hitching all over Santa Cruz. I'm not certain that he can't climb the fence at The Mansion if he chooses. He definitely needs to be contained."

Nick whispers to me: "Your dad isn't 80. He's only 70."

"He's actually 83-years-old."

Nick carefully scrutinizes Dad. "He doesn't look it."

I wonder how much of this Dad is taking in. His eyes look a little vacant again. He's asked to take the stand and to raise his right hand and swear to tell the whole truth and nothing but the truth so help me God. But what is truth to him at this point? They should say: "Do you swear to tell what you think you know as the truth at this point but may have forgotten or have confabulated to make things seem like what you want them to seem?" He says, "I do." He even puts in his hearing aid, which he normally resists wearing. He looks absolutely delighted to be sitting up there.

Tim asks him if he misses his car. "Oh yes," he says. "I love to drive, in fact right now I would like to go to Wall-Mart to pick up some things."

"Does Helen not buy you the things you want?"

"No, Helen buys me plenty of things, but I need to get my business taken care of. I have work to do."

"What kind of work? Is it not true that you have three years of taxes to file?"

"I have papers to take care of. Why are you asking me these questions? I have things to do."

Nick asks him: "Did you have a house in Marion?"

"Oh, yes. A lovely house in the country."

"How do you feel about it being sold?"

I cringe. Dad doesn't know about the house being sold. His eyes film over. "It's there. I need to get back to my work."

"How do you like Santa Cruz?"

"Oh, I like it very much."

It seems to me that Tim is asking questions that make Dad look bad, while Nick is asking questions that make him look good. Maybe, Dad knows which one is his lawyer after all.

The judge next asks Dad some direct questions. Dad again asserts that he believes he can manage his own affairs.

The judgment is given. He is to be conserved. "I won," he says.

I want to yell, "You idiot. You put us all through this for nothing. You didn't win anything but everyone's time." Instead I answer, "You did a great job testifying."

Dee Dee tells me that Dad can't stay there anymore. He has smeared the wall with feces and hit one of the caretakers. She stiffens herself and says: "Your father is a mean psychotic man. He should be someplace staffed by firm women who will keep him in line. He doesn't belong in a nice place like this." She gives me a new list of places to call. They extend from Los Gatos to Walnut Creek.

My father will have to leave Santa Cruz. We can't go out to lunch together and he won't be at our house for holidays or parties. If staying in Santa Cruz means that he ends up in a chemical straight jacket like some of the people in the places we visited, then it is best that he goes.

I decide to talk to one of the two women who are his primary caretakers. Jo is at the front desk and I ask her: "You heard about my father?"

"I sure did. It's too bad. I wish I had never put my mother in here. Sometimes I think she would have been better at home. She might have died burning up her trailer, but this was not a good situation."

"I know what you mean. It's really hard. What kind of place do you think would be best for Dad?"

"I'll tell you. One with more men and not so many women. He gets into his knight in shining armor routine, trying to rescue all the ladies and causes more trouble. I think he needs to be around more men."

"Thanks. That's quite perceptive. I'll see if I can find a place like that."

Jo puts her hand on my arm and looks in my eyes. "I know how hard this is. I like your dad. He's a great guy. I'm sorry."

Tears well up in my eyes. "Thanks. You've been wonderful."

In the car I'm tuned to different radio stations in my head. One is playing a poor me song about what I am going to do now and the other is airing a song of gratitude and tenderness for people like Jo who are out there on the line every day. They work long hours with little pay and yet remain sensitive, perceptive and open-hearted.

A cold and rainy Monday in November, Dad is standing by the door of The Mansion. He has on a light linen suit and a yellow fishing cap. He looks adorable, dressed for a summer holiday. "You're waiting for me," I say.

"Of course, I didn't want you to forget who I am."

He can still laugh at the disease which has changed so much of his life. "You look like you're dressed for a tropical vacation. Want to go to Tahiti Dad?"

"That would be great. You know your mom and I went to Tahiti."

"Did you like it?"

"Sure," he says with enthusiasm. "We were with a group of hot shot executives from big companies. They liked Charlotte and me and invited us to their cocktail parties."

He and Mom always did meet interesting people. On one trip to the Virgin Islands they hung out with Dr. Spock. He admitted to them that he had made a mistake in his earlier books. He had written that babies should be fed on schedule, and he now believed that they should be fed on demand. Too bad, since my parents used that book as their bible.

We eat at Fresh Choice, and Dad piles his plate with almost everything from the salad bar. Balancing the vegetables, he's able to create a huge mountain without spilling anything. We're quiet. He concentrates on eating and I'm thinking that he'll soon leave the Mansion and I won't have this time in Santa Cruz with him. I'll miss our lunches together.

Dad needs to go to the bathroom, and I wait outside the door. Five minutes pass, seven minutes, eight minutes, ten minutes. "Hey," I say, catching the attention of a young man leaving the restroom. Was there an older man in there?"

"Yes there was."

"What was he doing?" After I ask, I realize that it's not an appropriate question. "He was washing his hands."

"How long has he been washing his hands?"

"The entire time I was in there."

I wonder if I should ask him to go back to the restroom to get Dad, when he walks out.

"Dad, are you okay?"

"Of course. Why shouldn't I be ok? You worry too much. I'm fine."

On Saturday when I visit the Mansion, a man is strumming the guitar and singing in the lobby. He looks sweet--maybe a little country, about my age or younger. Most of the residents are downstairs having crafts, but Dad hates cutting, pasting and coloring, so the singer is serenading only Dad and me. Dad reaches over and takes my hand. We begin to dance--a slow fox trot. He twirls me and catches my hand again.

I'm thirteen-years-old at the Sinai Temple. The adults are dancing but Dad is not dancing with Mom; instead, he is dancing with Belle Weinberg. Her face is flushed and he's smiling. I want to go home. I don't want to watch this dance and I find my mother and tell her.

"Go tell your father," she says. "He'll drive you."

I walk up to him and tap his shoulder. He stops dancing. "I want to go."

"Excuse me," he says to Mrs. Weinberg. "I need to drive my daughter home."

"She doesn't like her father dancing so the daughter interrupts him."

I'm not certain to whom she is addressing her comment so I look at the floor. Dad leaves to get his coat and I follow him.

Dad twirls me again and the music stops. He says: "Helen, you're a good dancer. The guitar player asks for a request. He starts a slow ballad ... "Clementine". Dad and I sing with him. Some of the other staff and residents come over to watch and join in the singing, but the man playing the guitar continues looking at only Dad and me.

As I'm leaving, one of the attendants, a small dark man with intelligent eyes leans against the building. He draws deeply on a cigarette and says: "Your dad is getting a raw deal."

"What do you mean?"

"He's not being treated well."

"Is he being hurt?" I remember my dreams, those nights I woke up sweating with images of him being brutalized, held down and anally raped.

"No. No one is physically hurting him."

Thank God those images weren't psychic messages that I should have acted upon. I'm relieved to tell the man, "He's leaving anyway."

"It's not his fault."

I drive away in the car watching from my rear view mirror as the iron gates with their sharp spears close behind me. What isn't Dad's fault, that he is smearing the wall with his feces, that he tried to hit someone who came into his room? He must be really mad, like a two-year-old is mad. I'm just as happy to have him leave there. I only wish I knew where he could go. He can't live with me. This is Myrrhia's last year of high school. I'd have to give up my practice. He'd be awake all night, would burn down the house or take off wandering. I see Mom in her hospital bed and remember her words: "Take care of your father." I'm trying to take care of him. I really am doing my best. I feel tears run down my cheeks, useless drops only going that direction because gravity pulls them.

The Senior Center once more provides me with a list of possible facilities to check out. Bill volunteers to visit a well-known one in Walnut Creek. We talk on the phone afterwards, and he says, "The place is large. Dad would have to share a room. He's quite territorial as you know."

I feel tired, hopeless, scared, all of the bad adjectives. My only response to Billy is a sigh.

"What about Dusty?" Billy asks.

"I've asked him to check out the Adobe House in Petaluma near where he lives, but he hasn't."

"Well, it looks like the ball is in Dusty's court. Hopefully, he'll come through."

"I'll try applying a full court press and see how that works."

I wait until the next morning to call Dusty. He and I are both early risers and we often talk in the morning before work. "Hi Dusty."

"Oh, hi Helen". I hear the carefree chords in his voice and am envious.

I sound heavy and flat. "It's about Dad."

"Yes. Have you found a place?"

"No. That's why I'm calling. Have you checked out the Adobe House yet?"

"I haven't had time. I called them but haven't gotten around to going."

"Make time. I've talked to five different facilities and visited three. Bill visited the one in Walnut Creek and it doesn't look good."

"They have an open house tomorrow and I guess I could see. The people I talked to on the phone were nice."

In my bossy older sister voice I respond: "You've had a week to find time to get there. Tomorrow sounds as good as any. Call me when you come back."

Dusty's report of the Adobe House is glowing. The man who built it had two grandparents and one parent with Alzheimers. Dusty says: "You first enter a door where a receptionist greets you. You're then given a numeric code which opens another door. Once inside, there's a circular hallway. On one side are the residents' rooms, while on the other side of the hallway are doors leading to a courtyard. If a resident wants to go outside, he can walk through one of these doors and then come back inside at any place in the courtyard. The best news of all is that the facility is new and Dad can have his own room. It's furnished so we'll only need to bring a few items."

The day before he is to move, The Adobe House calls and says that they have received Dad's medical chart, but he needs to be examined by a doctor before he can be admitted. I pick him up after breakfast and take him to see Dr. Nash, who examined him when he first came to Santa Cruz. Dad shows him the fungus growing on his feet. "That's not a big problem," says Dr. Nash. "Use this ointment." He then asks Dad to undress without suggesting that I leave the room.

"Do you want me to stay?" I ask.

"It's probably a good idea," Dr. Nash replies.

"Sure Helen," says Dad. "Maybe you can help."

He has difficulty unfastening his trousers, so I release the hook and unbutton his shirt. Dr. Nash says, "He needs to remove his pants and his underwear."

I help him step out of his trousers and then stand back, allowing him to pull off his underwear. I walk over to the desk and with my back to my dad and examine the rocks that Dr. Nash has collected on hikes in the Sierras.

"How long have you had this enlarged testicle?" asks Dr. Nash.

"I had mumps as a child. I think I had it then."

Dr. Nash calls to me from across the room. "Did you notice it before?"

I look over at Dad and see that he has one very large testicle. It is so large that it dwarfs the other one. I think about calling out: "Hi big balls," but don't. I somberly respond: "Truthfully, I don't think I've looked at his scrotum much; but if I did, I don't remember it being that big. He's had his prostate removed so I don't think that is the problem. I have his 30 page medical history from Indiana Medical Center and they don't mention anything about his testicles in that."

Dr. Nash says: "You had some blood work done recently and everything was fine. If anything was wrong, it would show up there. You're in good shape for a man your age. You have the heart of a 30-year-old and the bones of a 20-year-old. You can get dressed."

I help Dad put on his socks, hook his trousers, button his shirt and take him back to The Mansion in time for lunch.

Later that afternoon Dad calls, asking when he will see me.

"I spent the morning with you at Dr. Nash's office. Don't you remember?"

"I don't remember going there. We did?"

"You were undressed and everything."

Dad sighs, "If you say so, I guess I'll have to believe you."

I'm shocked. We had spent an unusual morning together and Dad forgot the entire episode two hours later. I know that he often called me the day after Dusty or Bill drove down to Santa Cruz to take him out, to ask when they were coming, but until today I hadn't had the personal experience of being discarded from his memory. He forgot me. Someday, he may not even know that I'm his daughter. I know who he is and remember our history. I'll have to hold that love for both of us.

The next afternoon Dusty comes in his truck. Accompanying him is his 10-year-old son, Michael. I have asked Myrrhia to help. Michael and Dusty will spend the night at my house and move Dad the next day. Bill needs to be in court that morning and bows out. I buy a big pizza, aware that it may be the last time I ever have Dad over for dinner again.

This time is very different from when Dusty and I moved him from Marion, when Dad criticized Dusty's every move. He is even more relaxed than when he had to move from Sunshine Villa and actually compliments Dusty on his judgment and allows him some control in the decisions. Maybe Dad's good mood is because he is so happy to leave the Mansion, or the stage of his disease, or maybe it is because Dr. Gillette has taken Dad off the Risperdal and placed him on Buspar, a mild anti-anxiety medication. Dusty says: "Whatever he's on," pointing to Dad, "I want to be on it too. I've never seen him so mellow."

We caravan our cars to Petaluma. Dad is quiet on the way. I ask him how he is doing and he says: "Just fine."

PART 9
ADOBE HOUSE

The Adobe House is north of Petaluma in an area that until a few years ago was rich grazing land but is now being cemented into strip malls. The houses are built close together all from a similar prototype. Although the Adobe House looks like an apartment building and fits right into the bland persona of the surrounding area, I discover later that it houses some pretty unusual characters.

On entering the greeting area, Dusty instructs me to press a button. The director comes out, introduces himself. We follow him to Dad's room which has a single bed, a built in closet, a table and a bathroom. It's smaller than the one at the Mansion which was smaller than his room at Sunshine Villa. I like the fact that the room is well-lit and clean with few items to distract him.

We walk around the place and introduce ourselves to various staff members and some of the more alert residents. Dad says he is tired and wants to go back to his room and unpack. Once more, I leave him in a strange place. Dusty promises to visit him tomorrow and check in on him periodically.

It's nice to have Myrrhia with me. I have told her we will stop at Street Light Music in San Francisco on the way home, so she can shop for old vinyl and obscure tapes. "Is it hard to leave your dad?" she asks.

Some day I may be in my father's position and she might need to leave me. I don't want her to stop her life because of me. I answer: "Sure, but I think he'll be okay."

"Don't worry, Dusty will watch him. I know it won't be like having him close by but maybe you can have a break."

"You are one mature person Myrrhia. And I can spend some time with you now."

Dad likes the Adobe House. Again I am uncertain if it is because of the new staff, the Buspar, or the stage of the illness. Whatever the reasons, this is not a father I have ever known. Like during the old pre-Alzheimer days, he is caring and empathetic, but now he is calmer, allows others to take control, and he finds pleasure in simply being alive. When he was in Santa Cruz, I saw him three to four times a week. Because of the driving time to

Petaluma--two hours one way--I now see him every two weeks. I plan to take him out to lunch.

At the door to the Adobe House I press a button which alerts someone in an office inside. A voice gives me the five digit numeric code which allows me to enter. The code for today is today's date. I'm happy the codes are simple. I'm stirred up enough about visiting Dad without having to remember an unrelated string of numbers. I open a door and walk out on to a hall.

Dad isn't in his room, so I walk across the courtyard to find him. He isn't in the big recreational area either. I begin walking the circular hall. As I turn the corner I almost run into a man who I've seen before. He is tall and gaunt and walks with his head bent down watching his feet. His day seems to consist of continually walking these corridors. He follows the outline of the walls and when he reaches an edge, turns around and walks the other way. Someone said he used to be a surgeon. I've said "hello" to him a few times to see if he is interested in conversation, but he doesn't respond. I travel back to Dad's room and find him at the door, about to go inside.

"Hi Helen. What a great surprise."

"Do you want to go to lunch?"

"Sure."

"I need to sign you out." We walk across the courtyard to the recreation room. A petite young woman sits behind a window. She hands me a clip board. I write my name and Dad's and give it back to her. She hands it back. I look again. It turns out I have my name as resident and Dad's name as the "out person". Everything is still new and confusing to me. I wonder how Dad handles these changes. I correct the clipboard.

Dusty has suggested that Dad might like the Sizzler. On the way there, I ask Dad if he remembers Oatis Archie.

"Of course I remember him. He was your eighth grade social studies teacher."

I think to myself: He can't remember simple things, like how to dress but he remembers Oatis Archie.

Trying to watch the road and Dad's face at the same time, I continue. "I read an article about him. He was recently elected the first black sheriff in Indiana. He started out as a janitor, somehow qualified for the FBI and became one of the guards at the Rose Bowl parade. The paper quoted him as saying: 'I made it from the toilet bowl to the Rose Bowl.' In between, he must have been my teacher."

Dad's face has a slow smile crawling across it. "You raved to your mom and me about your teacher that year and we were interested in meeting him. You hadn't mentioned an important detail and on Back to School Night, we were surprised that the Marion Indiana school district was willing to hire a black teacher. We thought it wonderful that you liked him. Marion Indiana has so much prejudice. "We were proud of you. You know the Ku Klux Klan marched in full dress about five years ago?"

"Yes, I heard. I guess there are some things about Marion I don't miss. Do you miss living there?"

"No. I like going to lunch at the Sizzler."

As usual, he piles his plate high with items from the salad bar and we sit down to eat. Since we are already discussing the past, I decide to ask him about the Losantiville land trust, one of the items on the Conservatorship I can't trace. I've already written several court houses in Cincinnati, trying to track down this account. I have even called a place named the Losantiville Country Club. A young man had answered the phone and said that there hasn't been a land trust as long as he has worked there.

"How long has that been?" I asked.

"About 10 years."

"This may be longer."

Nick Wyckoff suggests that I might need to fly to Cincinnati to track the account. He warns me. Every single piece of information needs to identified."

It's a long shot but maybe he will remember. I look across the table from him, wait until his eyes focus on mine and say: "Tell me about the Losantiville land trust."

Without a moment's hesitation, he replies, "Let's see. That is a country club in Cincinnati. Your mom and I thought it was a good place so we bought a share. I think it was in 1938, the year we were married. The bank manages it. Call them."

When I return home, I call the bank and find out that for 60 years Dad has owned 1/10 of a piece of land in Cincinnati worth $40.38.

The next time I visit Dad, Dusty is at a wedding in Boston. Bill isn't speaking to me. I don't know why. He's never acted like this before. Because he isn't talking to me, he won't say what is annoying him. Since he has never done this before; I don't know, he will ever speak to me again. What will change his mind on this matter is sheer speculation. I send him faxes about Dad. The only communications from him are letters which he addresses to the William S. Resneck conservator. I would like to share my feelings and experiences about Dad, but he has made it clear that he wants no personal contact with me now.

I knock on the door to Dad's room and, as usual, there is no answer, so I enter. It's neat and tidy. Some cards from friends are lying on a table along with an odd assortment of magazines and brochures he's collecting. I decide to walk around the circular hall to see if I can find him. There he is.

I would recognize that stride anywhere. I smile but he walks right past me. Has it happened? Has he forgotten who I am? He used to drive past me on the way home from school, not seeing me.

Maybe it's that. The Alzheimers couldn't have invaded his memory of me. I call: "Dad, it's Helen."

He turns around looks at me for a few seconds. Does he not recognize me? Then he smiles. "Helen. Am I happy to see you." I hug him tight. Someday he won't recognize me. I'm glad it's not today.

"Do you want to go to lunch?"

"Of course. Let's go."

Linda, is in charge of the sign out clip board today. She's young and likes to tease us. "Hey Resneck. You're going to lunch. Bring me some."

"Sure," says Dad. "What would you like?"

"I'm just kidding. By the way, he needs a diaper."

"What?" I ask not certain I have heard correctly.

"He needs a diaper and a change before he leaves. I'll get you one. You can put it on him yourself or I can, but you should take one with you."

"I'll do it." After all she isn't his family and if she can change his diapers, so can I.

"They're in the closet in his bathroom."

I turn back to look at Dad and his pants are already wet. "I guess I'll have to change his diapers and his pants now."

"Your Dad is so funny. When his pants are wet, he'll walk down the hall saying, 'I need clearance.' It took us awhile to figure out what he meant."

I open the closet and find a box of "Depends". They're like disposable baby diapers but much larger. I pull one out and place it on the bathroom counter. I open the tabs of the diaper he is wearing and he steps out of it. It's wet and I'm relieved that I don't have to face the excrement of an adult meat eater or wipe his butt, at least not this time. I hold the clean diaper as he easily steps into it. I place it over his saggy scrotum and penis. As I fasten the tapes on both sides, I'm surprised how easy and natural all this feels. He puts on a dry pair of pants. Of course, I help him with the zipper. I decide to skip the belt as it seems too much to deal with. His shirt is wet so together we pick out a clean dry one. We end up with a blue shirt that makes his eyes glow like the sky at dawn. I ask him where he wants to eat.

Without hesitation he responds, "The Sizzler."

I find a table near the salad bar so that I can keep eye on him and allow him some time to hang out there. He slowly checks each item and then piles his plate high. I watch him eat. The salad has captivated his attention; and for awhile, he seems to have forgotten that I'm with him. He looks up and remembers I am there. A sweet smile widens his face and his eyes brighten.

My insides are like firecrackers. I must let him go. I must, because he is going.

After lunch we walk out to the parking lot. He looks at the car and says: "I forget how to get in."

I show him how to back up and sit down on the seat. One leg is pulled in and then the other. He imitates my gestures and says: "I forget things. I depend on you."

I respond without hesitation. "I will be dependable."

I walk with him back to the recreation room. There are pieces of paper to color with pictures of hot air balloons. I decide to sit and color with him. He's intense about staying in the lines. I make new lines and new designs on the paper. He says: "You color very well. They will be proud of you." I know he means his caretakers. Then he's tired so I walk him back to his room. I sit with him awhile. He becomes obsessed about the position of the bed and moves it a few inches from the wall, sits on it and then moves it back. I tell him each time I think it's fine, but he isn't comfortable and begins the procedure again. I try to distract him, talking about his friends in Marion, my brothers and Myrrhia, but he isn't interested, only focused on the bed. Finally, I decide to leave.

On the way out I stop at the director's office. I want to be certain they remembered the doctor's appointment I made for him last week. Turns out, they forgot it and don't have the records from his old doctor. On Monday I will have to to call his previous doctor to secure records, make another appointment with the new doctor, and call his psychiatrist to start him on Aricept, the new Alzheimers medication. I have hopes for this drug. Although it doesn't stop the growth of the plaques in the brain, it allows for more neurotransmitters to be available and might increase his performance. I hope that he will remember the mechanics of peeing for a while longer.

A couple of days later I receive a call from Nick Wyckoff. "We have everything lined up for the Conservatorship but we forgot to have his medical care listed."

"What does that mean?"

"That we have to go back to court again. It's my fault so I won't charge you, but it's something that needs to be done."

"He's in Petaluma. How am I going to get him from Petaluma to Santa Cruz court by 8:00 in the morning?"

"Hire someone to drive him down."

Thank God Dusty offers to help. They will drive down, spend the night and he will take Dad with me to court the next day. Dusty also agrees to wear long pants instead of shorts which is quite a compromise for him.

This time before court, I'm able to wake early and go for a run with the dog in the dark. It's nice to have Dusty along to help out. Before, I felt like a single parent with a handicapped child. He helps Dad dress, we eat a quiet breakfast together and head out to the county building. I introduce Nick and Tom to Dusty and to Dad again. He doesn't seem to remember either Nick or Tom this time or care which part they play in the drama.

Dusty sits on my left and Dad on my right. Dad asks a few questions in his voice that isn't a whisper. The lady next to the judge smiles at us again and I smile back. The judge reads the facts. He asks if anyone objects. All of the family members have been notified and no one has objected. No one is called to the stand to testify and the medical Conservatorship is granted. I now legally have the right to be in charge of Dad's medical well-being, which I have been doing anyway.

I wave goodby to Dad and Dusty as they drive back to Petaluma. He has no more authority over himself. The air seems still and quiet, as if some part of the fabric that makes the world, a background hum, has gone quiet. I imagine I hear a train whistle but know it's a memory from my childhood, when on a summer day that sound would remind me that someone is leaving.

This time I decide to bring my dog, Liat, to visit Dad. After he and I have lunch I plan to drive to Inverness to spend the night with my friend MaryAnne and her dog. As I drive into the parking lot of the Adobe House, Liat throws up all over the back seat. Luckily, I have a sheet down. It was originally for mud or sand that she might bring in, but handles her accident pretty well. She's happy now and bouncy. Bodily events are easy for dogs, and they always seem quite willing to pass on to the next adventure life presents.

My dad likes dogs and he is the only man that Liat has taken to immediately without reservation. She tries to bite Lily's father when he comes to pick her up after visiting my daughter. Liat won't even run with David in the morning, only me. But for some reason, she thinks my dad is fine. Instead of cowering and trembling like she does when she meets most men, she runs up and shoves her nose into his crotch. He takes this quite easily and gently pets her.

The love of dogs is something I've always shared with my dad. As a child, I was very attached to our dog, and the dog was attached to me. He slept in my room at night. I often found animals that adopted me and didn't want to go home. My dad patiently explained that we already had a family dog and didn't need another one. But I could see that he didn't want to send the dog away either. The animal was allowed to spend the night and I could give it food and water; then my father would run an ad in the local paper to find a home for it. We always charged $5.00. Dad said that if people were willing to spend some money for the dog, they valued and really wanted it.

Animals still follow me home. About ten years ago, when I was living in the Santa Cruz mountains, a horse began trotting after me on a run and came right back to the house with me. Last week, during a run a coyote trailed after Liat and me until I yelled at it to go away. Recently, a gorgeous pale green and blue parakeet alighted on my shoulder. I'd coaxed it there so I could catch it and find it a safe home. Afterwards, I sat in my back yard and started to cry. I felt like I betrayed the bird's trust. I called it to me only to capture it. I betrayed the bird like I betrayed my father. I convinced him to come to Santa Cruz and then locked him up.

I decide to try to bring Liat into the Adobe House with me to find Dad. At the second door we're stopped by a couple of staff members. One bends down to pet Liat while the other says: "Your dog needs a leash." She adds, "Your Dad is in the bathroom getting new diapers put on."

"You know," I say. "the last two times I have visited him he's been in the bathroom. He seems to pee often and in large volumes."

"He sure does," she agrees.

The other one chimes in, "But, he is a big man."

Dad's thrilled to see Liat and me and we decide to go to the Sizzler. We always act as if we might go someplace else, but it's the place Dad remembers and always chooses, so we go there. At lunch he saves some of his meat scraps for Liat. And in the car on the way back, he says: "We should ask the restaurant for other scraps. Then Liat would have enough not only for today but the day after."

Memories from the depression guide much of his behavior. When he was at Sunshine Villa and The Mansion, he hoarded bananas. When I picked him up from his home, his house was filled with fluorescent bulbs, jars, lawn tools that didn't work, magazines, newspapers, all of the family letters, love letters between my mom and him when he was in the army. They called each other "your little puppy" and "dearie".

On the way to the Sizzler he complains that people at the Adobe House call him "Dear". I tell him that I call David and Myrrhia, "sweetie". He says that he and my mother have never done that. I decide not to remind him of those letters I have found. But, he does agree if being called "dear" means they like him, it will be okay.

I take him back to the Adobe House and help him pull off his pants and diapers. He forgets again to hold his penis and starts to pee on himself. Without thinking, I grab his penis. It feels strange, soft and lifeless, like a partially deflated balloon. I drop it and he grabs it. Next time, I'll have him sit down.

When it's time for me to go, he follows me past the door with the code and out to the car. I put Liat in the back seat and walk Dad back. He won't let the door close and wants to know where I'm going and when I'll be back. I'd like to be there tomorrow. I'd like to take him back home with me. I wish he was still in Santa Cruz, where he could spend much of his time in my home. In reality, I don't know when I'll be back, but I tell him I'll be back in a week. He stands at the door and protests: "I can't stand here a week and wait for you." One his caretakers shuts the door. I don't know what happens to him next.

I telephone Dusty and he reassures me that Dad is fine. I won't see him again for another two weeks and try to concentrate on my work, thinking that will help me worry less about Dad. But, there's no getting away from it. Life has a funny way of providing me the opportunity to face my issues. For instance, the following week, Lisa a new client, asks if she can bring her partner, Joe, to the sessions. She wants to get married and have children but is concerned that Joe is unable to make a commitment to their relationship.

They choose to sit on the mat on the floor side by side. I bring up a low chair and sit across from them. Although facing me, they are quite aware of each other, and I watch their bodies weave. Sometimes, their shoulders touch and they lean into each other, or Lisa rests her hand on his knee. Joe looks at Lisa and with tenderness says:

"I love you but," he lowers his head and places his chin in his hand, "I'm unable to commit myself to anything right now."

"You seem ashamed to tell Lisa that."

"I am ashamed, but I also know it's not my fault. Is that possible?"

"Of course," I answer. "Often what we are ashamed about isn't our fault and then we can't make amends to change the situation. Instead it feels like our very self is bad."

Lisa leans forward to me. "He didn't do anything wrong." She pushes Joe's arm. Tell her."

"My mother died last year and I was her caretaker and her conservator."

Oh my god, I think to myself.

Joe clears his throat, lifts himself off the mat by his hands, sits down and moves his hips until he creates a nest for himself. He continues, "she was disabled and fighting with the hired nurses, so I decided to move into her house. I used her car to drive her to her physician's appointments and to buy groceries."

"You wanted to help your mother."

"He sure did," says Lisa emphatically, "but then Ralph... you tell her."

"Ralph is my oldest brother. He's a lawyer and was unhappy with the arrangement and felt that I was misusing her funds by driving her car and living in her house without paying rent."

"But he wasn't," chimes in Lisa. "He took care of his mother and they didn't help at all."

"That's right. I tried to enlist the support of my middle brother, Tom, but he refused to become involved." In a louder angry voice, Joe adds, "Ralph complained to the conservator's office and I was found guilty."

Finally, I think to myself, he's expressing some feeling.

"Because I don't have the funds to repay the estate, I'm required to perform community service."

As soon as he finishes describing the betrayal by his brother, he bows his head and folds his shoulders forward.

"You're angry and sad about this situation and feel hopeless."

"You're right." He sighs, "Mom died and Ralph still won't speak to me." As he begins to describe his mother's death, his breathing becomes heavy followed by wrenching sobs of grief. Finally Joe collapses against Lisa and she holds him. Afterwards he's embarrassed about showing emotion and apologizes to me: "I'm from Scottish people and we don't do this."

I notice that Lisa and I have matching smiles on our faces. She strokes his hair and I reply. "It's okay to mourn the loss of your mother and to be enraged with your brother. It seems appropriate to me."

After the session as I'm writing notes in the chart, I reflect on how generous both of my brothers have been about any money involved for Dad's care. Neither of them have questioned me; in fact, Billy was protective in discouraging me from bringing Dad to Santa Cruz without a Power of Attorney. When Dusty was sorting out Dad's possessions from the house, neither of my brother's were greedy and none of us fought over the possessions.

The drive from Santa Cruz to Petaluma seems to take forever today. I had initially planned to leave early in the morning. But when David found out I had scheduled a bicycle ride with Dusty, he wanted to come along. Sometimes, I think David would be more jealous of me riding my bike with another man, even my brother, than if I had sex with someone else. He finishes work at noon. Of course on the way out the door, Myrrhia has some last minute burning questions about a college application, and then there is the Friday afternoon traffic.

Still, we arrive at Dusty's house around 3:00 pm, with plenty of time for a bike ride and to pick Dad up at 5:00. But, Dusty isn't there. We check around his house for a note. But instead of finding out where Dusty might be, we stir up his dogs. Listening to their high pitched barking is maddening, and as we don't know why Dusty isn't there to meet us as planned, we decide to take off without him. As we begin to pedal away from the house, Dusty rides up on his bike. This countryside surrounding Petaluma is what I consider classic California. Covering the dry golden hills are bright yellow flowers growing on thick stalks. Although I'm pedaling hard to reach the crest of a hill, I find the breath to remark, "scotch broom grows easily here too. I've written an article about them."

He looks at the scotch broom and says: "Yeah, they aren't native plants but invaders from Europe like us who the purists want to eradicate."

"That is the point of my piece." I softly brush his arm as I ride past on my bike. Sometimes, it is so reassuring to hang out with someone from your family.

On a distant hillside we see smoke. Dusty talks about the dangers of fire up here, especially on a day like this with such high winds. When we ride up to his house and find it surrounded by fire trucks and hoses, we realize that it is the house on the hill above his home that has caught fire. The fire trucks seem to have it contained, but I feel a fist gripping my chest as I see the fire trucks and their hoses have trapped our car at his house. I hate to not be in control of my comings and goings, and now there is no way for me to get out and take my dad to dinner. Dusty calls the Adobe House and tells them we might be late. He asks them to try to stall Dad's dinner so we can still take him out. I don't know when we will arrive there.

Finally, Dusty's wife, Janet appears. She has rushed home afraid that it was their house on fire. She parked on the other side of the trucks and agrees to allow David and me to use her car to visit Dad. But we first need to take her back to the bank where she works. Dusty's friend has a car trapped too and he needs a ride downtown. Janet and Dusty stop to talk to the neighbors and share their worries about the fire. Although I'm concerned that it will be too late to take Dad out to dinner, I don't say anything.

As a young girl, I needed to be with my dad. On Sundays, Dad would take my brothers and me to Sutter's Dairy. This was the same dairy that delivered our milk each morning. They had a small section where you could use their ice cream, milk and chocolate to make your own shakes. Mom was waiting for us at home with peanut butter on Ritz crackers, my favorite meal. Sunday was Dad's afternoon with the family. But sometimes he had to go to work at Resneck's, the store he owned with his mom and brother. They sold women's and children's clothing and accessories. This was in the day before computers and he had to "do tickets". Everything that had been sold during the week had to be entered into a book. Sometimes, the whole family would help.

I remember one Sunday when he was going off to the store. I hid in the back seat of the car. Later I climbed out and knocked on the big glass door. He probably wouldn't have heard me except that my mother had noticed that I was missing and called him. I spent the afternoon playing on the adding machine.

Petaluma was a ranch community but is now being infiltrated by Marin County, and at rush hour, the traffic is gridlock. It takes a quarter of an hour to slowly inch our way to Dusty's friend's car. Then we have to negotiate several stop lights to the bank where Janet works. I try to calm myself that being late will be okay. Finally, we take off to see Dad.

When we arrive at the Adobe House, Dad has already started his dinner, but one of the caretakers insists that she'll get him. "He's my favorite person here," she says.

I think to myself: "He was one of my favorites when I was a little girl." He has on a yellow old man's cotton hat, the kind that they wear to go fishing. It's floral band clashes with the wool plaid shirt he's wearing. He reminds me of old men I used to see hanging around the lakes of Indiana and Wisconsin. I never imagined my father would look like one of them or that I would think he looked cute.

As always, we go to the Sizzler. He spends a long time studying all of the items on the salad bar. They are the same every time we come but always new to him. Then, he builds a giant plate of lettuce and vegetables with a banana on the top. About an hour into the meal he has to go to the bathroom. Luckily, David is there and manages it all. I don't think that I can take my father into the ladies room without permission from the manager. Until then, I can't take my father out by myself. I say good by while he's busy with his caretakers. I choke back tears as I climb into the car.

When my mother would be upset with us as children, my father would reassure her by saying, "it's just a stage. They'll outgrow it." I guess my dad has entered another stage.

I haven't talked with the manager yet about bringing Dad into the women's bathroom at the Sizzler, so for this visit Dusty suggests that I take him out for ice cream. As I enter the circular hallway, I'm greeted by Linda and another staff member I don't recognize. Linda asks: "You're here for Resneck, aren't you. He's in the bathroom."

"Is he in the bathroom a lot? I mean the last few times I have come here, that's where he has been."

The two women laugh. Linda answers: "I guess he likes it there." She yells. "Resneck, your daughter is here."

"Helen hi. I can't get this smell off my hands. I've been washing and washing them. The other woman says: "Is he still at that? I helped him wash his hands earlier."

"That's right," Dad agrees, "but I can't get this smell off."

"I have an idea. Let's replace that smell with the rich aroma of a hot fudge sundae."

"Now that sounds like a great idea."

We find a Baskin Robbins. He wants a specific flavor but can't remember the name. I suggest, jamoca almond fudge. When I went away to college and found out that there were 31 flavors of ice cream in the world, I sent away for the information on how to start a franchise and tried to talk my dad into buying one. My mother, Dad and I have always agreed that jamoca almond fudge is one of their best flavors.

We walk along the river with our ice cream. I ask how he's doing. He says he feels he has many blessings and has been extremely lucky in his life. He looks me in the eyes and says: "Especially the way you love me. You are special."

When my mother died, I knew that I would never be as special to anyone again. Until this moment, I don't think I ever really felt that special to my dad. "Thanks," I say. "I really love you, too." I wonder to myself, would he ever have been willing to be this vulnerable and open to me without Alzheimers? Our family is not usually sentimental and I start to feel anxious. I can't imagine where a conversation like this will end up. To change the subject I ask: "But how is life treating you?"

"I have worries."

"Like what?" I ask.

"Like the smell on this hand."

"Does the ice cream help?"

"It makes me forget about it." We both laugh.

I bring him back to the Adobe House but still have a couple of hours before I need to leave to meet a friend for dinner in Petaluma. Most of the residents are in the recreation room, so we go down there and take a chair. One of the caretakers yells, "Hey Resneck, you're back."

"I'm sorry," he says. "I didn't get you any ice cream."

"Next time," I say.

She and I sit side by side in chairs in the big recreation room. She looks at me and laughs, "The schedule says it's leisure time now."

"Yes," I say, "pretty stressful day for them here."

One of the residents toddles over to the piano.

"Watch your dad," she says.

He pipes up: "There goes the nun."

This woman begins to play throwing aside pages of the music book as she finds her way through complicated passages. I feel like I'm sitting in the middle of a concert hall.

"She used to play for the Mormon Tabernacle Choir. Your dad has decided she's a nun."

One of the residents, June, begins to cry. She entered The Mansion in Santa Cruz the same day as my dad. She was evicted the week before my father was asked to leave.

A waltz is playing and I reach for June's hand. "Lets dance." Her face lights up and we begin to move across the floor. I had dance lessons as a child and know how to lead with a waltz. I wonder if June had lessons too. I guide us over to where Dad is sitting and reach out my hand to him. "Don't you want to dance too?"

He smiles at me from his chair and says, "I'm too tired."

June pulls me back with her on the floor. I look at her face and it's smooth, free of worry lines. Dad watches us with a contented smile. The music ends and I sit next to Dad for awhile holding his hand. Again he says, "I love you."

I answer, "me too, but I've got to go." I kiss him on the check and then say goodby to everyone. On the way home I realize that I feel good about my dad, life, and my blessings.

Dad has been at the Adobe house for eight months. I wish that I could be more like my brothers and not worry about him and need to see him so much. Dusty says: "Don't you think that there is always one person in the family who assumes more responsibility than others?"

I guess I'm that person, but I also resent Dad. It has been almost a year and we still haven't been able to complete the first Conservatorship accounting. Tom at Dean Witter joked with my daughter today as I opened up a college checking account for her. He threw a huge stack of papers on his desk and said: "This your mother's file." I protested that that was my Dad's file, not mine, and that wasn't even all of his accounts.

This morning, the Adobe House called and said that Dad needed to talk to me. "Helen, is that you?"

"Yes, Dad, it's me."

"Oh good. They found you. Listen, I haven't been able to sleep. I feel my heart pounding at night and think about my death. I want your secretary to record that I want to be cremated."

"Of course, Dad." Although I don't have a secretary, I want to know his desires. "Do you want your ashes to be buried next to Mom in Indiana?"

"No, I want my ashes to be buried in your garden near you forever."

"I'm honored to have you with me."

He begins to cry. This emotional sentimental father is certainly not the one I have known most of my life. "Thank you Helen. That's all I have to say. I love you."

After hanging up the phone, I sit at the old oak dining room table and think to myself. Dad visited the emergency room in Marion only a year and a half ago and now he's talking about where he wants to be buried. Does he have a prescient knowing or is he receiving some somatic signals that he's dying? All of his tests at Dr. Nash's office were normal. Maybe it's only his awareness of having Alzheimers. I'm afraid to watch him slowly die. I've tried to talk with Dusty about the course of this disease, but he just screws up his face and changes the subject.

Dusty brought Mom's china from the Marion house and I sit at the table looking at the glass plates engraved with my grandmother's initials. After awhile the papers and magazines scattered on the table begin to annoy me. While making piles, one for David, one for me, and one for recycling, I hear a scraping sound at the front door.

Standing there is Myrrhia with a huge box. She has returned from Alfred University in New York where she spent eight weeks in the art school studying ceramics. "Look, my pottery came." She had to mail much of her work as the boxes were too big and heavy to bring home on the airplane. I help her carry it to the living room, and she begins to pull out pieces. I watch expecting colorful candelabras, pale pink birdhouses, building structures like the medieval city she built inside a castle, the kind of pieces she was making before she left for the summer. I'm envisioning the brightly colored mugs, vases and plates that had begun to fill my kitchen. Instead strange shapes and colors emerge from the box. She pulls out a perfect pot with a sandstone glaze. One side is pushed in. The small hole at the top looks like lips reaching. She next pulls out a tower of stacking canisters in a dull green and black color. The shine of the glaze offsets the drab of the colors. One pot has a top that has two flat spikes across the top. Finally she pulls out a pristine white pot with a rich purple glaze. She presents it to me along with a beautiful set of art deco plates and glasses.

"What do you think? Do you like them Mom?"

"I love these dishes and pots, but I have to say that I honestly can't relate to the rest. I miss your old pottery."

"This is art here. We had famous ceramicists teach us. My teachers raved about my work."

"I'm not an artist Myrrhia. I guess I miss the bright colors and whimsical pieces. I'm sorry I don't get these."

She also informs David and me that she has decided to attend the University of California at Santa Cruz. She glances at her acceptance letters from other schools and quickly tosses them in the wastebasket. I surreptitiously pick them out, if only to have a momentary feeling of pride in my daughter. Although she will be living in Santa Cruz, she wants to move out of the house. The dormitories look too small and confining for her and she has found a room in a co-op. David, her best friend Jessi and I help her pack up her things. All she is taking is her futon from the floor of her room, her desk and a chest of drawers.

The co-op is an old sprawling house, across from Sunshine Villa. A young man with a beard is sitting on the front porch playing a guitar. He sees us carrying in heavy loads but doesn't offer to help.

When I see her room, it takes everything in me not to yell: "No, you can't live here." It is filthy with pieces of dirt and other particulates of unknown origin on the carpet. The room smells like body odor with a faint aroma of cat pee. "Is there a vacuum somewhere. I don't mind sweeping."

"No, Mom, leave it. This is my room."

I look at the bathroom. Instead of being reassured, I notice an orange stain in the toilet bowl and the sink has disappeared below a blanket of debris. The kitchen counter is covered with food stains, orange peels and blackened pots. Myrrhia knows what I'm thinking. Usually when I start to worry about some problem in my head, she asks, "what is it?" I say nothing, but she always adds, "I can hear you thinking, tell me what it is." We're both smart enough now to know that this is not a good time for me to share my thoughts. Instead I say: "You could still spend tonight at home and sleep in the den."

"This is hard for me," she answers. "Don't make it any harder."

I kiss her cheek. "Put on a jacket, it's cold."

"I'm fine, Mom."

She and David have a long hug and then we leave. On the way home I thank him for being so accepting of her move.

"I'm not handling anything," he replies with anger. "I want to call the police and have her removed immediately." That night he tosses and turns, pulling the covers off me and then places them over me again. Finally, he leaves the room.

The next morning I find him on the living room couch. I kiss him and ask: "How are you?"

"Okay. I guess she survived the night and we'll just have to get used to this."

We go back to the co-op. Myrrhia is waiting for us on the front porch. She has agreed to go up to Petaluma to visit Dad.

After she has settled herself in the back seat I ask, "How did you sleep your first night in your new room?"

"Fine." I hear an edge of irritation in her voice. "You know how you don't understand the pottery I brought back this summer?"

"Yes," I say drawing out the word, cautious of what is to follow.

She's emphatic. "I've changed. I'm not your light little girl anymore. A part of me is dark and you need to understand, because that is who I am."

"Do you mean you're having sex, because I don't think of that as dark."

Exasperated she replies, "no Mom, I'm not having sex." She pauses and laughs. "Not yet, anyway, but I've changed. I feel different."

When we arrive at the Adobe House, Dad is so happy to see us that he begins to cry. Before I can mention the phone call about his ashes, he says: "I have to go to my room to pack a bag. I've been waiting for Dusty to drive me to New York to visit my cousin, Arnold."

"David, Myrrhia, and I have come to drive you to the ocean."

I don't know if he hears me or not but he goes into the bathroom to find his toothbrush and toothpaste. "Dad we're going for a drive. Maybe later you can go to New York but right now let's drive to Pt. Reyes and have lunch."

He turns around and faces me. His body slumps in disappointment. "I guess that will be alright." Dad sits in the front seat and Myrrhia is driving. The road to the ocean is curvy and Myrrhia takes some of the turns with tires squealing. I remind her, "You're driving a van, not an Indianapolis formula race car, slow down." She slows down for a few minutes and then speeds up again.

"Be careful to stay in your lane. Cars can cross over and hit you." She maintains what I consider a more reasonable speed for a while. Still, I'm not enjoying this ride at all, while Dad seems fairly relaxed.

That night I study Myrrhia's pottery. Odd forms metamorphosize into open graceful curves, much like Myrrhia's body. The glazes are no longer a blur and I see how blue becomes a pearly teal and then khaki. The browns are soft rusts and remind me of the rich colors of the southwest. I think to myself: Myrrhia has changed. She is a woman.

Dad has begun taking Aricept, the new Alzheimers medication. The drug doesn't stop the progress of the disease but increases the amount of acetycholine, the neurotransmitter fluid in the brain, so that the person can function at a higher level even though the sensitive brain tissues are being destroyed by Alzheimers plaques. I'm curious if the drug will have an effect on him and what that effect will be. I have arranged to meet up with Dusty to take Dad to lunch. He told me to call him from my car phone when I'm near Petaluma, but he doesn't answer. I leave my car phone number on his answering machine. I'm wondering if I am now being abandoned by Dusty as well as Billy. I try not to feel sorry for myself.

I find Dad in his room rustling papers. "Hi Dad."

"Boy, am I happy to see you."

"Great I've come to take you to lunch. I'll go sign you out."

When I come back and open the door, Michael, Dusty's youngest son jumps out from the bathroom and yells, "Surprise." Dusty says he would have called me back but he had received the typical car phone message: "I'll wait for your call at this number --s-c-r-r-r--static static static."

As I walk past Michael and enter the room, Dad launches into a tirade of accusations. He says that I have caused him to miss his Harvard class reunion by taking him on a drive in the country with my husband and daughter. He adds that I've also caused him to miss the planning of a big event at the Adobe House. I guess the Aricept is working. He's like the Dad I brought to Santa Cruz, crotchety, critical, and paranoid.

I'm not certain what aspects of the last visit are upsetting him. "Is it the drive that bothered you or were you angry that we took you away from the Adobe House?" He answers gruffly: "That is just a smart psychologist's reply. No, I want to go out." After much questioning I'm able to understand that he resents the long drive we took with Myrrhia, especially since he thought we were on our way to New York to see his cousin, Arnold.

At the restaurant he goes to the bathroom and comes out with his pants unhooked, falling down off his butt. He refuses to allow Dusty or me to help him fasten them. After lunch I tell Dusty to stay with him while I get the car. I don't want him to walk across the parking lot and have his pants fall down. By the time I return, Dusty has his pants secured, so we can buy some ice cream. Dad still can't remember the name of his favorite flavor, jamoca almond fudge, so I order for him. The ice cream and walk around the Petaluma river levee lift his spirits.

On my return to the Adobe House, I check with the staff about his recent behavior. Indeed, one day he did walk out of his room without any clothes because it was too hot. I'm reminded of when he locked everyone at Sunshine Villa out of the laundry room and took possession of the machines in his underpants. Carla, the director of the Adobe House and I agree that we should watch his behavior to see if he needs other medication.

For the first few days after Myrrhia has left the phone continues to ring for her. Once she has her own number at the co-op, the telephone quiets. I find myself enjoying this new silence in the house and don't turn on the radio or television. In between clients I walk out to the kitchen table and enter my notes in the charts. Noone is there to ask me questions. After I clean the kitchen in the morning, it stays clean all day. Myrrhia and I talk on the phone every other day and once a week she comes for dinner. I seem to have the best of both worlds, the house to myself while still having regular contact.

Today Marissa has scheduled a therapy session. About ten years ago we met regularly, but over the last few years she comes in sporadically as needed. She had a difficult time when her mother died of cancer. Not only did she deeply grieve her loss, but she's another younger sibling put in charge rather than the older brother. Her mother owned land that had belonged to her family for generations and wanted to be certain that it was protected against development. Her mother trusted Marissa to fight for that land, and I don't think she was aware of the emotional cost involved. Instead of setting up conditions regarding it's use in her will, she gave Marissa that job. The other siblings wanted to develop the land for profit and distanced themselves. Marissa's brother felt slighted and was so enraged that he hired lawyers to fight her. Not only had she lost her mother, but her family too.

I haven't seen her for awhile and want to separate my feelings about her family from mine. I not only love this woman but also respect her integrity and ability to fight for what she knows is good. Sometimes, it is at a cost to her own well-being. She tries to manage too much and suffers from a problem that my friends and I know well. We call it, FMS, "fear of missing something".

This afternoon, she's not only dealing with a divorce but is also is trying to decide if she can fly to New York, present a paper, come home, find new renters in four days for the cottages on her property, and then fly to Chicago for another conference. Her other plan is to fly to New York, then go visit her family's home in North Carolina, from there go to Chicago and lose money by not having tenants. While describing these plans I point out that she's having difficulty breathing and ask how the rest of her body feels.

Her curly hair softly frames her pixie face and I watch as her mouth twists and straightens as she struggles with a new plan; one in which she will not be able to pack in all of the events she desires. Once she reaches a decision, she plants both feet firmly on the floor and settles back into the chair. Years ago, she was plagued by debilitating asthma, but now she easily guides her breath to a soft regular rhythm. The muscles of her body smooth and a smile of pleasure rests on her face.

As we walk the path from my office to the waiting room, the dahlias seem to reach forward to brush her arm as she passes by. We say goodby. I expect I'll continue to see her from time to time over the years.

I'm making notes of the session in her chart when I receive a call from Carla. Now, it seems that my father has a girlfriend. They're walking around holding hands and at night take turns sneaking into each other's rooms. They were seen in bed together with her breasts exposed. The staff at the Adobe House is concerned because they are both Conservatees, not consenting adults, and of course my father is still legally married to Dorothy.

As my dad's conservator I give my consent for him to enjoy whatever sex he can with his prostate problems. Dorothy left my dad at the height of his paranoia and what she doesn't know won't hurt her. Besides, pretty soon both Dad and his present girlfriend will deteriorate and forget one another, and I add "if you resist it, Carla, well you know where that leads."

"I know," says Carla, "but her family isn't involved and I don't know if her son will consent."

I think to myself: What a thing to try to make a fuss about. Let them enjoy their pleasure. But aloud I say, "But she likes it."

"Yes," says Carla. "She likes your dad. We'll see how it goes."

"I'll see you at Hawaiian Day this Sunday."

"Good," says Carla.

David and I dress in our wild flowered shirts and drive to Petaluma. Lunch and games are provided for the residents and their families. I'll also have a chance to meet my father's new friend.

We find him seated at a table with his girlfriend next to him. I try to pull up a chair in between them but she maneuvers me out of the way. She's pretty, well-groomed, and very polite. "Hello," I introduce us, "I'm Helen, Bill's daughter, and this is my husband, David. What is your name?"

"Hello," she answers in a smooth polite voice. "My name is Doris. How old are you?"

I tell her and then ask, "how old are you?"

She smiles at me and says: "My mother knows." She leans over to my Dad. "You ate all of your rice. Would you like me to bring you more?" That was about to be my line. She's attentive to my father and I'm amused that we both want to serve food and perform the womanly tasks to ensure that everyone is comfortable at the table. David engages Dad in conversation.

Sitting at the table next to us is a woman who looks like she came out of the washing machine wrinkled and shrunken. Only a few hairs remain on her head. She begins to cry as her family leaves, so the staff seats her at our table. I ask her if she wants dessert. She makes a sound that might be yes, so I begin to feed her. One of the staff members stops by and asks me: "How were you able to convince her to eat?"

"I didn't know there was a problem. I put the food on a spoon and put it in her mouth. She did choke a bit, so I gave her some water. Is that okay?"

"Did she speak to you?"

"She made sounds that might be words."

"We didn't know she could speak."

I stop to sit with another woman and discover that she is 97 years old. She seems fairly sharp to me.

Later I take my father aside and ask him how he is getting along with his girlfriend. "Pretty good but I don't like it when she tries to feed me. I tell her, 'I'm not your baby."

Maybe she's just showing affection."

He shakes his head slowly and says: "Maybe so, but the other problem is that she doesn't have a very good memory."

I don't know what to say to that.

Janet, Dusty's partner shows up. She convinces my dad to enter coconut bowling. David and I say good by to them as they are throwing a coconut at bowling pins.

My life has become quite busy which makes it difficult to visit Dad. I have returned from leading a therapy group at a conference in San Diego and am grabbing this free day to visit him in Petaluma. The next weekend I'm going to Los Angeles to the Bar Mitzvah of Carol's son and then to Oregon to a conference. Seeing Dad every other week seems like too much. After all, he may be there a long time. I'm committed to being a steady visitor, if not such a frequent one. After this trip I don't plan to drive up to the Adobe House for another three to four weeks.

David says he wants to go with me to Petaluma, but when I return from the farmer's market he's turned off the water to fix the front bathroom which hasn't been working all week. I decide to leave without him or even a shower though the dog and I went for a run earlier in the morning. I also notice that I have misplaced my wallet. I drive back to the farmer's market but no one has found it. I go ahead to Petaluma without it.

Dad has on a pair of shorts that are falling off his butt. He agrees that a belt would help, and I rummage around for one in his closet. I watch Dad thread his belt through the loops of his pants. I'm impressed that he is now able to perform this task which was impossible for him a few months ago. Yeah for Aricept.

Sitting on his table is a letter from my brother Bill addressed to him. I open it. It is a legal paper asking that he and Dusty Resneck be provided with any documents filed in Santa Cruz regarding Dad's assets. If he had called me, I would have provided him with this information. He could have told me that he was filing this document instead of sneaking behind my back as if I was purposefully withholding information from him. I'm surprised by his behavior. My head is hot and my eyes burn, then ache. I want to scream in rage, why are you treating me this way? Is this all that is left of our relationship? A wave of sadness flows over me. I don't want to cry in front of Dad but he notices my shock. "Why do you look so sad?" he asks.

"Oh just stuff at home," I tell him. I don't want my upset to spoil our visit but am near tears. "Let's eat," I say.

He walks out to the parking lot carrying the letter from Billy in his hand. "I want new shorts now," he insists.

I try to explain to him: "I don't have my wallet. I can't buy you shorts." He starts to throw a temper tantrum insisting that we go to the office, that they are holding his money and that he has an account with them. This Aricept may be helping his thinking, but now we are back to the Santa Cruz temper tantrums.

I look at the car and notice that my trunk isn't shut. I open it up and sitting on the ledge is my wallet. I jump up in the air and yell "Yahoo". Dad laughs.

"Boy," he says, "you sure can be happy."

"Yes, Dad. Happiness is a great thing to share. Unhappiness I'm not too certain about. We can get shorts, but let's eat first. Do you want to go to the Sizzler?"

"That's a good place."

He has a difficult time getting into the car. His back hurts. I ask him, "Do you think a roll to support your lower back would help? It always seems to help me when my back hurts."

"We could try it."

I run into the Adobe House and find a towel and roll it up. I help him place it behind his lower back and he says he feels better.

When we reach the restaurant I convince him to let go of the letter and place it under the front seat of the car. Once inside the Sizzler, I look for a comfortable place for him to sit but all of the booths are taken. I point out a wooden chair with a hard back and he says it will be fine. Looking across the table at him, I notice how blue his eyes are today. My stomach is so tight from finding the letter that I can hardly think about eating.

Dad again says my eyes look sad.

"I don't want to share my unhappiness," I say. Although I'm furious with Billy, it seems unnecessary to bring Dad into this family feud.

"Come on," Dad says. "I'm here for you."

Once again, I feel tears well in my eyes. I make up a story that I'm unhappy about something that is happening to David. Dad seems satisfied.

He decides that he is too uncomfortable getting in and out of the car to shop for shorts. He feels ready to go back to the Adobe House. This is the last time I see my father standing.

The next week I fly to Oregon with my friend Judith for a conference. We have traveled many places, both physically and psychically. Our paths first connected during bioenergetic training. We shared the same therapist, and our daughters became friends. We commiserated and challenged each other through marital separations, divorces, and illness. She lives in Menlo Park, so we meet up at the airport. As always, she is casually elegant in a black jumper and white blouse. She doesn't need to wear colors as her red hair takes care of that. On the plane ride I tell her about finding the letter in Dad's room. "What do you think Bill's so upset about?" she asks.

"I don't know if it's about me or Dad or both of us. I called Dusty to see what he thinks about the letter, but he didn't call back. Nick Wyckoff says that it's a common document for lawyers to file, to ask for a full disclosure of assets. But I have to wonder if that is all that this is about. I would be happy to give him the information, or he could have warned me about this. There's something aggressive in his behavior and I feel it."

"Helen, I don't know either. It's definitely aggressive, and unfocused behavior. I'm not sure if he knows what he's so stirred up about. It must be hard to be the oldest son, and a lawyer, and not have the power."

It's a week after my visit with Dad and I have just returned from Oregon when I receive a call from Dusty. "Hi Helen." His voice is quiet and somber and sounds like he's only playing the left hand of the piano keys. "Dad's in the hospital. Bill and I arrived at the Adobe House to take him out to dinner and he couldn't stand up. He had to be taken in an ambulance. We waited around to make sure that he was okay.

They told us there was nothing more that we could do so we went home."

"What's wrong with him?"

"They don't know. They're going to do some tests."

"What's he like?"

"He's okay."

"I'll drive up to see him tomorrow."

The next day is full. In the morning my friends Blair and Carol have invited me for a dog walk by the ocean. Then David and I will attend an open house where Aaron works. After that we'll drive to Petaluma to visit Dad. Dusty is giving Janet a fortieth birthday party in the evening.

Before meeting Carol and Blair, I usually run with Liat. This calms us both so that we can walk at their pace. While running, I watch the waves as they break in ten foot glassy rolls. I want to swim in them but am worried about being alone in surf that large. I continue running until I find two adolescent boys on boogie boards riding the waves breaking closer to shore. One has brown skin and the other is fluorescent white. They both shine and glisten as the water surges beneath them. I swim out watching the waves and take a few mellow rides. The powerful surge of the water pushing and pulling against me matches the tidal swell of anger and grief welling up inside. I want to swim out to the big break and I call to Liat to join me. She looks at me for a second and then slowly backs up as if to say: "You're nuts, I'll watch you from the shore." One of the boys says: "Your dog is telling you the water is too cold. It's too cold for me too." I watch the boys glistening like seals as they head to the shore and think to myself, I could stay in here forever. I feel warm and supported and I love this sensation of being held and dragged by the water.

I check my watch and it's late, so I run back up the beach with Liat in front. She turns around and heads toward me. She's found Carol and Blair and their dogs. "You sure look like you're enjoying life," says Carol. "Are you part mermaid?"

"Yes, as my dad says: 'Life is good. Enjoy these precious moments'."

Dad is lying in bed with an IV attached to his arm. He has a heart monitor taped to his chest and is fidgeting with it. His head is cocked at an angle. It looks really uncomfortable. David says: "Hi Bill."

Dad opens his eyes, sees David and says his name with delight. I walk over to the bed and plant a gentle kiss on his forehead. "Oh, Helen, I'm glad to see you." He closes his eyes. I ask him if he wants a drink of water. He seems to be dozing and doesn't reply. I try to move his head, but he winces.

"Do you think he's in pain?" I ask David.

"Maybe, it's hard to tell."

"What is causing him to sleep, the drugs or his condition?"

"Probably both."

"I walk over to Dad and look closely at his face and gently take his hand in mine and hold it.

Dusty comes in with Michael. He walks over and says: "Hi Dad. Do you want some water?" With the same moves I have just made, Dusty tries to adjust his head. Dad once again winces in pain so Dusty backs off. Dad begins repeating the phrase: "The unhappiness can't be shared." He says this over and over. Dusty looks at me.

I know Dad is repeating the last phrase I said to him at the Adobe House when I found the brief Bill had filed. I don't want to go into all of this now with Dusty so I say: "I guess it's best not to share unhappiness."

Dusty begins to ask David the same questions I have asked. I wonder about how Michael is feeling, seeing his grandfather in bed hooked up to an IV. I give him some bubble gum from my pocket. Dusty comes over and takes Dad's hand. He has repeated the identical sequence of gestures that I just enacted.

"You know Dusty, I came in and offered Dad a drink of water, asked David the same questions and then tried to adjust Dad's head."

"You have to do something. I don't know, you have to do something."

We all sit together watching Dad.

After awhile Dusty stands. "I have to go. I need to pick up ice and charcoal for Janet's party. Are you coming? I have a belly dancer as a surprise for her."

I can't believe that he's pulling this off. His dad is in the hospital and he's putting together a birthday party for his wife.

"Sure. We'll try to come."

In his sleep Dad complains: "I have enough socks."

No kidding. Dusty has ordered him a box so he now has twenty-four pairs of them. He wakes up and asks me to comb his hair. As I gently move the comb through the one side of his head that is available, I sing to him lullabies from my childhood. In a sweet voice he says: "Hel bell." I'm surprised and look at my husband and say: "Noone has called me that in years."

David wryly answers: "Noone else but your father would dare."

In the car on the way to Dusty's house, I ask David: "What would you want if you were in Dad's condition?"

"To be taken out with morphine."

"Right," I say. "I wouldn't want to be tortured with needless tests. I don't want to have to deal with a lot of pain. Get me out."

I'm not in a party mood but am appreciative to Janet for all of her help and caring with Dad and want to help her celebrate her birthday.

We park down below Dusty's house and start up the hill. I think I see Billy's car but I don't want to wait around to see if he will recognize or shun me. I walk ahead but a voice yells out: "Helen."

It doesn't sound quite like Bill and I turn around to see Michael. He must have been riding in Bill's car. "Hi Michael," I yell back. I slow my walk and he runs to catch up with me. As we near the house, David turns around and says hi to Bill. He apologizes for not seeing him. They're friendly and talk awhile. Bill asks questions about Dad's medical condition. He doesn't acknowledge me nor I him. I leave the birthday party without either of us speaking to the other.

The next day I talk with Dad's physician in Petaluma, Dr. Jewell. "Your Dad's x-rays show holes in his spine, and his blood tests indicate that he is losing calcium. I think this is some kind of cancer and am consulting with an oncologist. We need more tests."

I ask, "will these tests hurt him?" I can only imagine the pain he must be experiencing with holes in his spine.

"We will keep him well medicated," he reassures me.

After hanging up, I pull out Dad's living will. He has checked that if he has a brain disease, he does not wish to undergo chemotherapy. Well, that is clear, but it doesn't say anything about performing the necessary tests needed to diagnose his condition.

I can't shake the image of Dad in bed, moaning with an IV tube stuck in his arm. The telephone rings and it's Karen, the nurse from the Adobe House. She calls to ask me how Dad is doing. I have to tell her that he doesn't seem well and I don't know when he will be returning to the Adobe House.

"That's too bad. I really enjoy Bill. One night the residents had the flu so some of us staff were up late washing the bedding. Your dad couldn't sleep so I told him he could stay up and talk with me. He related the story of how he came to America."

"Oh really."

"Sure, Bill said he was a miracle baby, that he had been adopted during the war by German parents as a play thing for their children. Isn't that wonderful?"

"That's a great story but in actuality his father left Russia when 12-years-old to escape from being drafted into the Russian army. Jewish boys were sent to the front lines and killed. So Dad was actually born in this country."

"But he was so convincing."

A few days later I receive another call from Dr. Jewell. This time he says that Dad has tumors all over his body. He's uncertain of the diagnosis and needs to run a few more tests. However, Dad won't be able to return to the Adobe House and he's probably dying. Somehow, I'm not surprised. I don't know how Dad could survive and have holes in his spine. With the Alzheimers he has been dying in slow states, and now his body is finally catching up with the deterioration in his brain. I wonder if this will be a slow painful illness and am concerned that his pain is managed.

I promised Karen, that I would let her know the specifics of Dad's medical condition, so the next morning I call the Adobe. House. Shannon, one of his caretakers answers and I tell her that Dad is not coming back. She repeats: "Oh no, oh no," several times. "I can't imagine not seeing Bill. Oh no." She wants to come visit him.

I call Dusty. He talked to Dr. Jewell today and tells me what I already know, that Dad has tumors and holes on his spine and that he's dying. Dusty adds: "I visit Dad every day. Yesterday it was time for his ultra sound. The technicians were angry. They told me a couple of days ago Dad grabbed one of the men and wouldn't let go. Do you know what I said? I said to them: "That's my dad." While I was there, they tried to move him and Dad yelled at them to stop and made a fist."

"See," the technician said.

"Do you know what I told him? I said, 'Yep, that's my dad.' Then I took hold of Dad's hand and talked with him in a soothing reassuring voice. His body quieted and the technicians were able to transfer him from the hospital bed to the gurney to the van outside of the hospital where the procedure took place."

"Was he medicated? It sounds like he's in a great deal of pain."

"I guess. I don't really know."

Dusty calls. He had gone to the hospital to visit Dad and found Karen in the room crying. She apologized, saying that she had come there to offer support and didn't think she would cry.

"I told her it was ok to cry." He adds: "I love life. Dad loved life. That is what makes this so hard." He starts to cry and I cry on the phone with him.

It is October 8, 1997. I am cooking dinner. Because El Nino is causing the water temperature of the ocean to rise, I am serving ono, a fish usually found only in the warm waters of Hawaii. It was caught off the shores of Santa Cruz. I call to Myrrhia in the garage, which is also her ceramics studio, and tell her dinner is ready. She is listening to the radio while checking her pots because it is supposed to rain. The announcer says everyone is breathlessly awaiting "El Nino", the WORST STORMS OF THE CENTURY. They are broadcasting it like a horror show.

She looks up at me and says: "Mom, the trade winds have switched direction. The last time this happened was in 1982. That was the year when your mom died."

We were living in Ben Lomond at the time and it rained for days until the mountains came down in a huge mass of mud and trees. Aaron's and Myrrhia's school was trashed. People were killed. It was right after my mother died. I guess it's time for Dad to die; the winds are blowing in reverse.

When my mom was in the hospital with leukemia, all the nurses adored her. I remember a particularly awful scene. Her veins had collapsed due to the continuous transfusions to replace white blood cells, so they had placed a catheter in her shoulder. She was telling a young resident it hurt. He was standing across the room yelling at her. Because her white blood count was so low, people were not to come close so as not to contaminate her with germs. The fear was that she would die from an infection. I was secretly crawling into bed and holding her.

This doctor was telling her with some disdain that all catheters hurt and that pain was just part of the procedure. In exasperation I finally said: "Why don't you look at it."

He hesitated.

I said: "How do you know her pain? Look at it."

He took off the bandage and gasped. Her shoulder was swollen, hot, and badly infected.

When my dad had his hernia surgery, no one from the hospital came to say goodby. He had been assertive, even demanding, but at seventy-four, he was alive. My mom was dead at sixty-seven. Dad is an impulsive aggressive fighter, especially when he is scared. My mom became philosophical.

I hate to admit this. My mom died fourteen years ago and I still miss her. I wonder if I will miss my dad that much. I don't think so. I was part of my mother's body. As an infant my nervous system tuned to her like a violin. When she died, I forgot appointments, lost items of clothing and spent days staring out the window. I'm glad I don't have to watch Dad slowly die from Alzheimers, like my friend Blair's mom. She died because she had forgotten how to swallow.

David walks in the door from work. I kiss his cheek and give him a hug. "I'm glad you're home. I was afraid you would miss the call."

Janet has arranged to meet with the oncologist and call us from the hospital room. Because David is a doctor, he can help interpret the oncologist's report and will know what questions to ask. I put the pasta into the pot to boil and the phone rings.

I reach for it and hand it to David. I walk into the other room and pick up the extension. Dad's doctor begins: "I can't give you an exact diagnosis of your father's condition. It is most likely a cancer. More tests would only cause your father needless pain to diagnose a condition that isn't really treatable."

I understand what he is saying but ask the age old question, just to be sure: "What would you do if it were your father?"

"Sometimes that is a difficult question to answer, but not in this case. Call hospice."

Janet has been in the room with the oncologist and I know that she has listened to at least his end of the conversation. After the oncologist leaves the room, she takes the phone and I ask her what she thinks. "I know he said that your dad is dying, but are you sure? He could be wrong. Maybe we should have another opinion." It is not so long ago that her father died and I know that she cares about my dad.

I ask her: "You are in the room with Dad. Is that what you truly believe?"

She sighs and I hear a tremor in her voice. "No. I'll tell Dusty."

"We'll have to find a nursing home. David and I have a friend here who works with the elderly. He can give us a list of the ones that are good in Petaluma."

I hang up and say to David, "Janet seems upset. To me the oncologist confirmed what Dr. Jewell has been saying. I wonder if this is the first time that she has heard that Dad's illness is terminal. I've been grieving all week. Actually, I feel like I've been losing Dad since he had Alzheimers."

David opens his arms and I rest my head against his chest. He strokes my hair, and I close my eyes and feel his warmth and the steady rhythm of his chest rising and falling with each breath.

Dusty calls to tell me that he fed Dad dinner tonight. "It was like feeding a baby. He made tiny fists with his hands. Before at the Adobe House he was like a toddler, walking down the hall with toilet paper attached to his pants."

"He did what?" I ask.

"One time he came out of the bathroom dragging his toilet paper. He thought it was cute."

If he is an infant now and a toddler at the Adobe House, what was he in Santa Cruz?"

Dusty responds without hesitation: "A rebellious teenager."

"He sure was, running around trying to get hold of a car, defying authority. To change the subject, have you found a nursing home?"

"I want him to stay in Petaluma, but I haven't found one."

"Have you looked at either of the two we heard are good?" I remember how I had to push him to look at the Adobe House.

"I'll visit them tomorrow."

Back to a full court press. "I want Dad out of the hospital where he can receive better attention."

He promises to visit them tomorrow. I decide not to wait for him and will begin calling some of the good ones in Santa Cruz.

Myrrhia wants to say goodby to Dad, so I make plans for her to visit that Sunday. She has always been close to Dusty's oldest son, Jacob, so Dusty and I arrange for them to go together. It is a gorgeous October day. David decides to take the coastal route and cut over at Half Moon Bay. I enjoy watching the sun's gold fragments reflect off the blue water, but my body feels weighty, like I could just mold myself into the car seat and become a fixture.

We open the door to Dusty's house and are greeted by Jane, Dusty's first wife and Jacob's mother. On the one hand, I am happy to see her; and on the other, realize that I don't want to be with a group of people at the hospital. I arrange to go first, to have sometime alone with Dad.

He has been moved to the transitional care unit which is down a long hall through a door and down another long hall. Lines of pain cover his face and every time he moves his head, he groans. I stroke his face and talk quietly to him. He opens his eyes but they don't focus on me. I spend about an hour alone with him and he never comes into consciousness.

I find my way down the long hall back to the nurse's station and ask what it says on his chart. She explains that he is only to have pain management, and she didn't give him any medication today because he's sleeping.

I go back to his room and sit for awhile longer. He seems to be in pain even though he is sleeping--sleeping or has his brain entered another state of consciousness? I sing a Hebrew song to him. He stirs and says: "I always loved that prayer."

I start to say, "me too," but my voice cracks into sobs.

The bones of his face are elegant. His cheekbones are prominent and his cheeks sunken. He is still a beautiful looking man. I don't think any of my parents' children matched them for beauty. But as I gaze at my father's profile, I am struck by how much he looks like Myrrhia. She has his regal bearing. Even at eighty-three, nearly eighty-four, his skin is still lovely.

Myrrhia and David enter the room and then Jane and Jacob. Jane tells Dad how much he has meant to her and how she has felt his guiding presence in her life. She tells him she loves him and I say: "He loved you too." And again I break into deep sobs of grief as my daughter reaches her arms out and holds me. So much has changed. My daughter provides support for me as I have been dependable for my dad.

I walk the long hall back to find the nurse. She is at her station writing in charts. I clear my throat, say, "excuse me", and wait for her to look up. She catches my eyes and looks down. I continue. "Even though Dad's asleep, we all see that he is still in a great deal of pain."

This time when she looks up she continues to make eye contact. "He has orders for morphine. I'll give him some right away."

I follow her back to the room. She gives him a morphine shot in his mouth and he shouts out clearly: "Don't do that to me." I'm happy to hear his strong response. I sit with him a while longer and watch his face contort with waves of pain. I return to the nurse and tell her that he still seems to be in pain. She calls the doctor and he is now to be given morphine intravenously every three hours. His legs are mottled up to his knees. Death is coming soon. I imagine huge strong wings with glossy white feathers pushing out of his torso, lifting him from his hospital bed. I wonder if, given enough morphine, he will be able to fly.

We return from the hospital to Dusty's house. I sit on a wooden bench on his back deck which overlooks an expanse of green lawn. In the distance lie brown dry hills. I wonder how long Dusty plans to let Dad stay in that dark corner of the hospital.

He's been declared as not needing further medical treatment and will die, so the staff isn't particularly interested in him. I need to get him out of there.

"Dusty," I say his name firmly in order to have his attention. "I have been nagging you all week to reserve a bed for Dad in a nursing home. I can't take this much longer. It's time to get him out of the hospital. He needs his pain managed which hospice will supervise. If you don't act today, I'll take him home with me."

Janet comes from the kitchen door to the deck. "How are you going to take him out of the hospital and where will you take him to?"

"I'll lie him down in the back of the van. If a nursing home isn't available, I'll take him to my house until one opens up in Santa Cruz."

"You're willing to do that?" Dusty asks.

"Yes I am. I can't stand to watch him suffer."

Jane is new to this situation with Dad. She puts down her beer and asks Dusty,"why haven't you decided on a nursing home?"

"I have. I just need to call them."

Janet says, "call the place now." She turns to me, "don't worry, we'll take care of your Dad."

Dusty goes into the house and returns within minutes. "I've reserved a bed. I'll see that he is moved tomorrow."

I return to Santa Cruz trusting Dusty to follow through on his promise. Although at this moment I am furious with him, like most encounters with the men in my family, there is no further conversation. Resentments linger for awhile and dissipate. The arguments remind me of milk weed plants. Their pods are stuffed with seeds tied to filmy tufts. They open and explode into the air waiting for a wind to scatter them afar. A few weeks later most of the evidence of milk weed has blown away.

PART 10
A FLASH OF WHITE

The afternoon of October 14, 1997 at 5:00 I leave the grocery store and am placing my bags in the trunk of the car, when I feel something at the edge of my body. The gold light of the sun shifts. Out of the corner of my eye, I see something white. A flash appears so briefly, I am not sure that it happens. A chill goes up my spine. Grief hits me so hard that I fall over on the groceries and start to sob. To let loose in the grocery store parking lot is not okay with me. I look around but no one has seen me. I open the car and slouch in the driver's seat ready for whatever is coming, but the gripping sadness isn't there. It seems to have left as suddenly as it came.

On entering the house, I check the answering machine. It has a message from Janet. "Your dad probably won't make it through the night. You're welcome to come now and stay with us. Dusty is still at the nursing home."

I call her back but there's no one there so I leave a message. I call David. I'm going. I leave a note for my clients on the gate into my office. It says that there has been a death in the family and I'll call to reschedule appointments. I climb back in the car heading straight to Petaluma. Highway 17, the curvy mountain road separating Santa Cruz from San Jose is beginning to straighten and become 880 when the car phone rings. "Hello. It's David. Your Dad died. Janet called."

"He died just now?"

"Yes."

"I'll call you back." I pull off the freeway and punch in the numbers. As soon as I hear the click, I ask, "he's dead?"

"Yes. Are you coming home?"

"I don't know, I mean I don't think so. I'm over highway 17 now. Maybe I'll go to Petaluma. I don't know. Let me figure this out."

I sit in the car for awhile, start to cry and stop myself again. Something isn't right. The world feels unreal. In fact I haven't felt three dimensional reality since I was in the grocery store. I start driving north. The air is warm and the sun is setting. I remember driving in the car late at night with Dad. After he had recovered from his collapse in the hospital in Chicago, we resumed that family vacation driving to California. He refused to call ahead for motel reservations, so we often drove until we could find a place to stay. We drove through the starlit desert, Mom and the boys asleep in the back, Dad and I in the front, content to enjoy the warm dry air and the silence of the purple night. I notice that I'm nearing the Dunbarton Bridge. I could cross over to Highway 101, stop driving and spend the night with my friend, Judith; or I could drive on up to Petaluma. I pass the turn off to the Dunbarton bridge and think, that's it I will go to Petaluma. My eyes ache. My eyelids and head feel so heavy. Maybe I'm exhausted. At the next exit I turn around and head for the Dunbarton bridge toward Judith's. But I don't even know if Judith is home or whether I should go there. I call her.

"Hi Judith. It's me, Helen. Dad died."

"When?"

"Tonight."

"I'm sorry to hear that. Where are you?"

"I'm on the Dunbarton Bridge. Can I come over?"

"Of course."

She is waiting on the porch and gives me a long hug. I breathe in that good Judith smell, a combination of cedar and smoke. We sit in her kitchen and she brings out brandy--a good drug to distance and deaden life's events when they are too big.

I feel like I am confessing something foolish, but I sniff my brandy and say, "I loved my parents. They were like the main characters in the movie. Other adults were part of the supporting cast, but they were the hero and heroine. I watched them, followed their lead for awhile and then decided to go my own way, but they set the standard. Maybe everyone feels that way about their mom and dad, but I loved them."

"You, as well as I, know from our work, people have different feelings about their parents, but your parents were big people."

Anabell her sixteen-year-old daughter comes into the kitchen. "I'm sorry about your dad. Is Myrrhia okay?"

"I don't know if she's been told that Dad died, but I'm sure she will be fine."

"Is it alright if I tell you something? Jonny my old boyfriend called. He wants to talk about his new girlfriend, Marie, like I really want to hear about his new girlfriend. Why do boys do that? They all want to tell me about their girlfriends but that doesn't feel very good." Annabell continues to talk quickly but the amazing thing to me is how coherent and perceptive she is. I haven't seen her in about 6 months and she has grown. I find her monologue a welcome relief, and Judith and I exchange knowing laughs.

The next morning Judith and I take a walk. We visit a little shop that opens to a garden with ceramic art objects. It's good to be reminded that life goes on, but I don't feel totally connected. I'm observing myself walk, the sunshine shines more gold and orange than usual; the grass is greener. Sounds seem to travel from far away and then suddenly are near.

I leave Judith's house with the plan to take 280 to 101 to Highway 1 to Petaluma. Instead, I cross the Bay Bridge and drive through San Francisco. Each section of the city is an experience. I taste the metal of the bridge and the Chinese food simmering in pots. The blue of the ocean is a sharp contrast against the orange of the sun. I think about Dad's body. It will be burned up. The life of the senses is gone for him. I want to put something of mine in with him. Then I'll put his ashes in the garden as he asked and it will all be mingled together. I don't have anything in the car I and I packed my bag in a hurry. As usual I've packed running clothes, so I'll put in my old favorite triathlon t-shirt, the yellow Brannon Island one. It is one of the few races I came in first, not that it mattered to him. He never showed any interest in that aspect of my life or really in the garden. But the t-shirt will do. I've treasured it for years because it's yellow, so it's good to put something of value with him.

As I approach Petaluma, I call Dusty's house. Bill answers the phone and says: "Hello Helen." I am shocked. He hasn't spoken to me in months. Maybe he feels there has been enough grief. I hope that Billy and I can be a family again. Dusty, Janet, Billy and I drive to the funeral home in one car.

Chapter 11
The Funeral Parlor

We enter the funeral parlor. The room is dimly lit and we can barely read a a sign that says: "Please sit on the couch." There are two long leather couches. None of us move toward them. I look up and notice the ceiling is high with deep texturing. There are raised areas in the room underneath a round dome in the ceiling. I taught in a room like that in Toronto last year. It was a chapel and whenever I stood beneath the raised part of the ceiling, my voice echoed and I felt like God talking. We stare at the couches for a while longer and then a man ushers us into another room. Although he is quite a bit younger than the four of us, his dark suit and starched white shirt gives him an air of authority. He introduces himself as Mr. Dumstead and sits behind an enormous deck. It is spotless and empty, without one piece of paper on it.

Janet quips: "Behind in your paper work."

This room is also dimly lit and there is one couch with two chairs near his desk. Janet, Dusty and I sit on the couch while Billy, the eldest brother, takes a seat near the desk. Dad has died which ends the Conservatorship. Bill has been appointed executor of Dad's estate, so he is now in control of the finances.

He says: "I guess I'm up at bat next."

"Yay," I yell in the funeral parlor. I realize my enthusiasm is unsettling to everyone at that moment, so I explain myself. "I'm sorry Dad died, but I have to say, I am grateful to be released from this Conservatorship and Dad's 300 accounts."

Mr. Dumstead clears his throat and begins. "I have some questions that by law I'm required to ask. First," I want you to know that there are four crematoriums available. They all do the same thing. One has a bad reputation, so it is cheapest. The other two cremate a small volume of bodies and are the most expensive. Finally, there is one in Marin. Marin County has a lot of cremations so this makes it cheaper."

"Is that kind of like the Wal-Mart of crematoriums?"

"Yes," he says and smiles. I see that he is able to appreciate our humor and not hold a posture of grief-stricken seriousness. "You could describe it like that and by the way, call me Jerry."

"That's the one I think my dad would like." My brothers agree.

Jerry writes some things down on the one piece of paper which he retrieved from the top desk drawer. "OK, next," he says, "there is how your dad is to be transported to the crematorium. We used to transport everyone in cardboard. But now there are regulations and you have several options. We have a cardboard box, a pine box, an oak box..."

Dusty interrupts. "The cheapest. We want cardboard."

"No," Janet protests. "You can't send him in a cardboard box."

"I think I'm with Dusty on this," I say.

Billy nods his head and says: "Me too."

Janet is horrified. "You can't."

"Actually," I say, "I think my dad would really like "the boys", my brothers to pick up his body and put it in the back of Dusty's truck and drive him to the crematorium in order to save money."

"He'd have me out looking for a refrigerator box right now to put him in," says Dusty.

"So, it's cardboard," says Jerry.

Janet's face gathers itself into a mockery of worry. "I don't know if I can forgive you guys for this. This is like going to the funeral parlor with Woody Allen's family."

Jerry begins to read from a piece of paper. "You need to be aware that all of your father's gold fillings, jewelry, clothes any items he now is wearing will be cremated with him."

No wonder Jews were against cremation after the holocaust. I have a vision in black and white. Men in gray cotton suits are picking out the gold from the teeth of corpses. Large smokestacks loom in the distance against a gray drizzly sky. I quickly push that picture away and think about my dad.

"I don't think the shirt he is wearing is his shirt," I say trying to remove the bleak images.

"Yes it is," says Dusty. "Don't you remember the blue shirt with the bear on it?"

"I don't think he ever had a shirt like that."

Mr. Dumstead says, "It happens. Once we had a funeral for a lady. Her things arrived from the nursing home, including a little embroidered pillow. Written on it in silk thread was the sentence: "We love you Grandma". Someone saw the pillow in her casket during the funeral and was horrified. She never had any children."

Everyone is quiet for a few minutes. I break the silence.

"I know this is weird but I have one other request. I want something of mine to be cremated with Dad."

"What is it?" Billy asks.

"This is not a well thought out decision. When I received the call last night that Dad was dying, I packed everything in a hurry. All I have is an old triathlon shirt." I hold up the shirt.

"Can she do that?" Dusty asks.

"Sure, let me tell you another story." Jerry begins. "One time a man wanted to bury a can of beer with his grandfather. When he was 10-years-old his grandfather had caught him drinking beer. Instead of telling his parents, he had sat down with him, shared the beer and talked to him about problems associated with drinking. So, he placed a beer in his grandpa's casket. During the funeral as they lifted the casket, they heard this clank pop, pow and beer began oozing out the sides of the casket. Needless to say, the mourners were quite frightened."

"Do you want to put something in with your dad?" Janet asks Dusty.

"No that's okay." He gives me that I've got a weird sister look.

Now it's time for the "viewing of the body". I want to touch him and stroke his cheek one last time. Janet warns me. "Helen, this isn't going to be like you think it is. He has been in a cold room overnight. He may not feel like you think he will."

"I hear you. I get that it might be hard for me. Thanks."

Dad is stretched out on a table, his eyes closed. He is wearing the blue shirt with a little bear on the left. My dad's face was always alive with animation and movement. His face is still and the skin is tight, emphasizing his prominent cheekbones and aquiline nose. He looks regal. I stroke his hands and feel his soft skin. I outline the bones of his cheeks, as if to memorize with touch and vision this face I have known all my life and will never see or touch again.

After the others leave and I am alone with him, I pry one eye lid open to see if his eyes are still the same intense blue as when he was in the hospital. They have returned to their gray blue softness. I pass my hand near the top of his head and feel a slight warmth. I wonder if it is like the Tibetans say, that it takes awhile for the soul to leave the body and find its way out of the top of the head.

Soft crying sounds emerge from my mouth. Slowly the sounds begin to change and gather up into a full wail of rage. I am surprised at my own reaction. I will not allow myself to scream. I think I should be relieved that he is free from pain, but I am angry that he is gone. I want to see the smile that lights up his eyes as I enter the room.

We return to Dusty's house and he and Billy set out a bottle of vodka and tomato juice. I bring up the topic of the funeral. We decide that we will have a service in Petaluma. I think that we should also have a service in Marion, where he lived the last 60 years of his life. I wonder if Dusty and Billy are interested in coming.

Billy announces loudly: "I'm not going to Marion."

"You're not?" says Dusty astonished.

"I'm only asking who might want to come." I am surprised that my voice sounds so calm. I guess I'm not as shocked as Dusty by Billy's response. I know that he is embarrassed by Dad's behavior in Marion and doesn't want to be bothered with a difficult and expensive plane flight. It costs more to fly to Marion, Indiana than to Paris, France.

Billy looks at me and says that he will think about it.

Dusty brings out bagels and cream cheese. He reaches into the cream cheese container with his fingers. I'm about to ask him to use a knife and realize that it's his house and our father just died, so it shouldn't matter.

"You know," begins Bill. "Dad really doesn't want a funeral. When I was in Marion last time at the grave site, he told me to sneak in and dig up the place next to Mom and bury him myself."

Dusty is licking his fingers and about to put them back into the cream cheese. I pull it away. "That sounds like one of Dad's good ideas. Was that before or after the Alzheimers?"

Dusty yells, "what are you doing?"

"Use a knife."

Billy pours himself another drink and continues. "That was the problem. He was so quirky how could you tell. You all remember Mr. King, Dad's janitor at the store. I went down to the basement once and Dad was on the ladder and Mr. King was watching while he changed the light bulbs."

"Do you remember," adds Dusty, "when we tried to lift the desk with Mr. King and all four of us couldn't do it. Then we looked down and Mr. King had his foot on the bottom. It was so heavy because he was standing on it."

I also refill my glass and add, "sounds like Mr. King and Dad were a good match. What I could never figure out is how he knew if someone came near his top dresser drawer. In between his socks, he stowed little plastic toys for us. Sometimes, I carefully opened it, looked at the contents and shut it. I didn't touch a thing, and yet when he came home from work he would ask: 'Who was in my dresser drawer?'

Dusty finishes off the last of the bagels and closes up the cream cheese. "Do you think he had it jerry rigged?"

"How would he do that?" I ask.

Dusty stands by the porch door. "He could have put a little piece of paper on the drawer and it would have fallen if anyone opened it."

I can't imagine that he would have gone to all that trouble. "Do you think he would have done that?"

105

Billy and Dusty look at each other and laugh at me. Dusty is almost out the door as he says, "let's go for a walk."

"Wait," I yell, "I need shoes." Dusty has already started slowly up the hills. I slip on my shoes and run after him. We slow down to allow Billy and Janet time to catch up. The sun slowly and gracefully lies down on the hills below. On the opposite side the moon begins to rise. It is an enormous red ball, which looks too heavy to ever rise up in the sky. It seems to grow out of the hills. It is Libra, the time in which the moon and sun are in balance with one another and the night of the full moon.

Chapter 12
The Mourning Period
Sitting Shiva

The yhertzite candle sits on the ledge in the living room over the fire place. It is red and reminds me of the red moon I left behind in Petaluma. In the early morning I see its bright flame and think of my father. Twice a day David and I say the Kaddish, the prayer for the dead. When Myrrhia is home, she joins us. I know the words from my childhood, "Yit-gadal v'iyit-kadash sh'mey rabah. B'almach di-v'rah chirutey. Exalted and hallowed be God's greatness in this world of your creation." The candle will burn for a week. I know my dad is dead, I saw his body in the funeral home, but it feels like he is still dying. According to the Tibetan Book of the Dead, it takes awhile for the dying process to be complete.

It is October 21st, the last night of Shiva and Billy's birthday. My brothers and I have a tradition of calling each other to wish a "Happy Birthday", but I'm too angry with him to do it. It is also my cousin Alice's birthday. Yesterday I missed her call. She left a message on my answering machine about Dad. I call to wish her happy birthday.

"I'm sorry about Uncle Bill. He and I were close. I talked to Bill and he says that he doesn't think he can go to Marion for the service because of Rachel's involvement in soccer."

Rachel, Bill's 10-year-old daughter is a soccer star. "That's interesting," I tell my cousin. "I guess I shouldn't go because my daughter was valedictorian of her class. I think there is more to this, but I can't say I understand it all."

I hang up the phone. David and I say the Kaddish before the last dying ember of the candle. It flickers and sputters as Shiva is about to end and then the glass holding the candle cracks and shatters. The light from the candle is gone, my father is dead, and I don't want to talk with my brother on the night of his birthday. I want my dad.

David goes to bed, but I can't sleep. I stare at the fireplace. Finally some time early in the morning, I begin to sob. The grief flows into the huge glowing globe of a moon that hovers in the sky that night. The next morning I am calm. Billy's birthday is over and tomorrow would have been Dad's eighty-fourth birthday.

Chapter 13
The Petaluma Funeral

We arrive at Dusty's house a little early. Janet is busy in the kitchen and Dusty is fussing with the drinks. Michael and Jacob both saunter into the kitchen. I say, "hi guys," and their faces break into huge grins. I'm reminded that Dusty won first place at Camp Dick Runyon for having the biggest smile.

Dusty suggests that I take Jacob and Michael with me to the funeral home to pick up the ashes. Myrrhia, Aaron and Siobhan want to stay and help Janet with the food. Although Michael has not lived in Petaluma for a year and doesn't even drive, he knows the way to the funeral home. Aaron was like that too as a little boy. We leave the bright sunlit day and enter the dark funeral parlor. Jacob wants to know why they have a case displaying china. I don't have a clue.

A man brings a plastic box of Dad's ashes. He is pale and soft and speaks in a hushed voice. I look at Jacob and he and I start to giggle. Then I look at Michael and notice the solemn expression on his face. I compose myself for Michael and so does Jacob.

The man hands me the box and its weight pulls my arms down. I knew it would be heavy because I had carried David's father's ashes. But this box is as big as five encyclopedia books and as heavy. I then remember that Dad was a tall man which means a lot of bones.

Michael wants to carry the box and I hand it to him. On the way to the car he asks: "What if I drop it?"

"If you drop it, you drop it, but you won't do that Michael." I remember how critical my father was with Dusty.

Jacob asks me to remove the orange parking guards his father has placed to prevent anyone from parking in the driveway. Our car carries the ashes and he decides that qualifies it for driveway parking.

Janet wants the ashes hidden. After the holocaust Jewish law decreed that no Jews could be cremated. They didn't want any holocaust survivors re-traumatized by the idea of their loved ones being burned in ovens. Now that time has passed, it is once more allowed. Still, Janet is spooked by the idea.

She and Dusty have arranged an altar for Dad. They display his awards. There are pictures that Janet took the last Father's Day. Karen, the nurse of Adobe House has brought pictures showing David and me with Dad on

Hawaii Day. Included is the photo album of the "Book of Memories" I made for him when he first came to California.

People start to gather. I'm happy to see that my cousin Jim, Uncle Dan's son shows up. I know he was angry with my dad around their division of assets. I'm happy to see that he has been able to put his anger aside and has come to mourn with us. At the funeral everyone has a chance to speak and I hope he decides to say something.

The rabbi is a short woman, a little over-weight and dressed in a black suit. Her soft green eyes look at me with kindness. This is my first experience with a rabbi who isn't male. Because we are mourners, she needs to ask our permission to touch us. After saying a Hebrew prayer, she pins a black ribbon on my brothers and me which designates us as "the mourners" to the community. She instructs us to tear a little bit of the ribbon which represents the tearing of the clothes in grief. We all say the Kaddish.

Because Bill is the eldest, he is invited to speak first. He walks into the center of the room, as if it belongs to him. He describes Dad as a young man always striving to emerge from the depression and win at the "making money game". He felt that he didn't see much of my father until Dusty and I brought him to California.

I read a cheesy poem that I hurriedly wrote the night before. I'm happy to have something written to read, as I don't think I can be extemporaneously coherent.

EULOGY FOR DAD
10-18-97

I'm 4 years old, wake up
from the tonsillectomy calling for him,
My Daddy, my daddy.
These last few days feel like a dream.

I want him to wake up, to feel his cheek
his warm hand enveloping mine as he says,
Gosh your hands are warm.

My dad grew up during the depression
and never had enough.
He was always checking the bill
and haggling the price.
While working in college, he spent his first month's salary
on a pair of shoes that didn't fit.

They were too small, so I grew up wearing
shoes that were always too big.

He taught me to drive a car, balance a check book,
fill out college applications.
He almost didn't make it to my wedding
because his back went out.
Everyone went to his motel room to help him
but me. Although he missed the rehearsal dinner,
he came to the wedding. I have a picture of him kneeling
in front of Aaron, my step-son, my only son.
He told Aaron from that day on,
if he ever needed anything to let him know.

He helped Aaron with his math and gave him
his first watch, complete with 23 functions.
I thought of him every other week,
as I reprogrammed it.
Myrrhia, at three, so enthralled, fully dressed
followed him into the shower talking.
Later, he listened to her opinions and philosophy
of life, just as he listened to mine.

Dad sobbed with me during ET, the hospital scene
reminding us of Mom's dying. And the next year,
realizing he had never held and loved her enough,
he cried in my arms again.

He went to Harvard on a scholarship.
did all the right things to stay healthy
no coffee, little alcohol, low fat, lots of vitamins and
died anyway, as we all will.

Last week I saw him lying in the hospital bed,
He moaned in pain and said my words of the week before,
"My unhappiness can't be shared."
I leaned into my daughter's arms and
sobbed for my daddy, my dad.

I walk back to stand in between Myrrhia and David. He squeezes my hand and Myrrhia draws me near into a hug. I look at Janet. She is smiling with tears running down her face.

Dusty walks up slowly. He looks very serious. "When I was little I fell down the basement stairs. I wasn't hurt but was badly frightened. Dad held me. Even now, I remember his arms and how I felt safe and loved. And as Dad died, I held him in my arms." Dusty begins to cry.

I fell down those same stairs with a similar experience.. I send him a smile, but he doesn't smile back. Dusty likes to mock feelings that he considers as too sweet or serious, but not today. I look over at the pictures. I'm drawn to one of Myrrhia and Michael, smiling with Dad in the middle. Janet took that picture on Father's Day. Dad was at the Adobe House and we all met in Petaluma. I didn't know that it would be the last Father's Day.

Jimmy stands up to speak. His white hair and blue eyes made teachers want to cast him as Jesus in the school plays. Even though Jesus was Jewish, Aunt Barbara and Uncle Dan didn't think it was right for him to be the star of the Christmas play. He begins to say a few words and then is interrupted by sobs. He's an opthamologist for Kaiser and has always been the rational scientist in the family. I've never seen Jimmy cry, not even as a boy. He composes himself and begins to speak of Asherwood, the 100 acre woods Dad and Uncle Dan bought anonymously and donated to the Marion school system. But he breaks down and has to stop, and it takes several attempts before he recounts the story.

Janet says that she wants to speak. She walks to the center or the room and says, "Bill had a wonderful sense of humor. He was always one for a joke." She pauses, looks around. I smile at her. Then she starts to cry and walks away saying, "but I can't think of anything funny right now."

That is unusual for Janet. She always has a quip or a funny remark. I want to put my arms around her, but my legs are rooted to the carpet. David drops my hand and walks to the center.

"Bill encouraged me to be more confident about my skills as a doctor and to go into private practice. He was a great support. But what intrigued me was that he drove a made over police car. It had special springs and a suped up engine. I wondered if he had a fantasy life as a secret agent."

He walks back to me for a kiss. My head and legs seem to be tied up and it takes a great deal of effort to move my head so that my lips lightly brush his cheek. The idea of Dad having a fantasy life or any kind of internal world was something I had never considered. Of course, he would have to be the hero.

Reed, Irma and Milt's son talks about how my dad had the most beautiful translucent skin. He was interested in others and asked Reed questions about himself. Dad had an insatiable curiosity and was always willing to engage with someone.

Of course like all Jewish events, after the ceremony we eat and talk. Janet invites us to come for their house for Thanksgiving, but I need a respite from visits to Petaluma. As we leave Dusty's house, I think about asking Dusty for the Book of Memories but decide to leave it with him. I have enough memories inside that I don't feel I need the photos, except for one. It is the picture of my mother lying on a dock in a bathing suit. Her hair is free to blow in the wind and she looks happy. Dad said it was the day he asked her to marry him. Later I'll ask Dusty for that picture. Now, I just want to go home and lie down and be quiet.

I wear my torn black ribbon on a black jacket all week. I don't want it to be too visible to my clients, but I wear it as a reminder. In the morning when I dress, I think about my brothers and wonder how they are feeling and if they are wearing their ribbons. When I find myself enveloped by intense waves of grief, I feel the ribbon and remind myself that I am a mourner. It is expected.

The next Sunday Myrrhia comes to fire her kiln and spend the day. In the afternoon she and I take a walk downtown together. We go to several music stores and listen to CDs. We then visit all the stores that sell hand made jewelry and California art. We marvel at the pottery. We encounter two of Myrrhia's friends and for the first time I notice what she is wearing.

"Are those Dad's clothes?"

"Yes."

She has on Dad's yellow hat. Lately when he put it on he had said that he could hear the radio waves that controlled Adobe house. I ask Myrrhia how it feels to wear it.

"Fine."

"Not hearing anything?"

She laughs. "Just hectic signals, well not really. It only works for Grandpa."

"Are those Dad's pants and shirt?"

"Yes."

I see Dad's face grinning at me as I find my wallet on the ledge of the trunk and yell: "Yahoo." My father's high cheekbones and oval face fades and reappears as Myrrhia's broad smile under the yellow hat.

When I tell my cousin Jim that I'm angry at Bill, he says it will someday be a blip in the history of our relationship. I think, a blip, like on an electrocardiogram, the blips are the beating of the heart. They tell us we are alive. It is the flat lines that are dangerous.

When I was 4-years-old, I loved to swing out as far as I could on the bar at the top of the sliding board in the park. It was as if I was flying. When I let go of the bar, I landed on my butt, and swooshed down until my feet hit the ground at the bottom of the slide.

One morning, Billy came to the park and I wanted him to see that I could reach out further on the bar than anyone. "Look at me," I called to him. His face turned up and his eyes were big and scared. I heard him yell "stop", so I let go and fell to the ground. Worried faces huddled around me and I was taken home. My mother gave me chicken soup, which entered my stomach and turned into a whirlpool. A little while later it ended up in the toilet, almost in the same form I swallowed it, complete with tiny bits of chicken. The doctor said I had a slight concussion and to keep an eye on me.

The night after Jimmy talked about the blips, I have a different dream about that day. Billy tells me to let go of the swing, just like that morning in the park. But this time instead of hitting the ground, I fall into my father's arms. He is young again and carries me to my mom. We are having a family picnic. Mom gives me a glass of lemonade from the big jug. I run off holding Billy's hand. Dusty is a baby and has to stay with Mom.

Chapter 14
The Marion Funeral

On November 1997, David, Myrrhia, and I leave the house at 4:45 am to drive to the San Jose airport to catch a 6:30 am flight to take us to Marion, Indiana for the final service. We are all half asleep. My brothers have given me permission to keep a small portion of the ashes for my garden, and the rest I'm taking with us to be buried next to Mom. I'm afraid I'll forget or leave them somewhere and continually ask David if he has remembered Dad. As we fly over the flat snow-covered land, I remember a similar flight in November. I was so over-whelmed with sorrow, I couldn't imagine that life could go on without Mom. We fly the same landscape, but this time carrying Dad's ashes for his funeral.

Dusty has said there are many variations of gray in the Indiana winter sky. This is one of those days. I drive the rental car through the flat land from Ft. Wayne to Marion. Myrrhia is hungry so we pull up at a grocery/deli next to a restaurant with a gigantic painted chicken in front of it. Myrrhia positions David in front of the chicken while she takes his picture. Once in the car she laughs and says, "Seeing the sights in Indiana is always so exhausting."

We drive into Marion from the north side and not much has changed. In fact Marion's population hasn't really grown much since I left 33 years ago and may even be decreasing. I recently saw a special on TV which explained why the population of the town has been stable. It was about a lynching of three black men that took place in Marion in 1930. It was the last reported lynching in the United States. I had heard some rumors about a hanging but never knew the whole story until I saw the TV program. In fact, I was told that a Jewish man was hung in Marion; and to this day, I'm not certain if that ever happened. The narrator who was the only one of the three men who had survived concluded: "Marion must deal with its past. All of the towns around it have grown. But not Marion. There is a curse and it won't leave until the people of this town deal with this lynching."

As we drive into town, I tell David and Myrrhia the story of the of the black men and how they were lynched. I don't mention about the Jewish man.

The narrator was an elderly black man who is currently living in Milwaukee. It seems that two of his friends talked him into robbing a young white couple who were down at the Mississinewa River "making out". He described himself as an unwilling participant who reluctantly accompanied them. In fact, his family had good relations with the girl's family and she recognized him. During the process of the robbery, the young white man was shot.

The three black men were taken to the county jail and booked. The second night a huge crowd gathered at the town square. The sheriff said to the young narrator, "I know you are a good boy, and I'll see what I can do."

But the crowd burst in to the jail. First one black man was taken away. The crowd beat him with their fists and sticks, the women tore at his clothes and skin with their fingernails. Finally, a rope choked his neck and he was left dangling from the big oak tree in front of the courthouse.

The second man pleaded and begged for mercy, but he too, was pulled from his cell and dragged across The Town Square. Finally they came for our narrator. A couple of the men recognized him but still he was grabbed, beaten and dragged from the end of the rope to the square. A noose encircled his neck.

The old narrator paused. He said: "Suddenly it was very quiet. I filled my heart and all of my thoughts with God. I saw a brief light in the sky and for some reason, I don't know why, the crowd left. I walked myself back to the jail. Although I had been beaten by fists, ripped by fingernails, and dragged across the ground, there wasn't a bruise or mark on my body. I was in prison a year and then released."

The last scene of the TV show took place in a church in Marion. He and the family of the white boy who had been killed were on their knees together praying.

As I finish the story Myrrhia says to me, "So you know about prejudice. This is a true story."

"Yes. I know a lot about prejudice from growing up in this town, but I don't want to talk about it anymore. Let's drive by the river before we go to the motel. Is that ok?"

Christmas decorations line the bank of the river, but they aren't lit up yet. I remember that Marion has a Christmas tree factory. One night driving home from a semester of graduate school in New York, I took the wrong turn on the Ohio turnpike. Instead of heading west toward Indiana, I was driving east. It was snowing like crazy and I didn't know I had gone the wrong way until I saw a sign that said; "Welcome to Pennsylvania". Disheartened, but always having great endurance, I followed a snow plow at 35 miles an hour the other way through Ohio. I didn't reach Marion until 3:00 am. It was Christmas and from the east side to the northwest, the town was alive with lights and decorations. My mother was waiting up for me. "This town looks gorgeous," I said as I reached out and hugged her tightly.

"You've been driving too long," she said. "Go to bed."

115

As we enter the park, Myrrhia asks: "Don't you want to drive by the house? I'd like to at least see the outside and we're almost there."

I turn on the road to Shady Hills and answer, "I've been thinking about whether I want to see it or remember it the way it looked when I left with Dad. I've been told that the new owners have fixed it up. Let's at least drive to it and then decide whether we want to go inside."

It sits on a beautiful little rise and I stop the car in front. The two birch trees that had been in the front yard are missing. I knew they were diseased but I still want them there. The line of rose bushes that was the boundary between our house and the neighbor's vanished long ago. I was the one who pruned and fertilized them. I loved the sweet smell as I arranged them in vases in the living room, even though Mom was allergic and they made her sneeze. One of the fir trees is gone. I picked bag worms off that tree with my dad. The hillside of pine trees on the left was the view from my bedroom window. My mother provided the rooms with furniture and tasteful art. She served us lemonade on the back porch and held parties that were causally elegant. She died and Dad viewed the tables as places to mound stacks of paper. I start up the path to the front door and see a Christmas tree in the window. I know that it's not my home anymore and walk back to the car.

Betty Fleck and I have exchanged e-mails. She is one of Mom's friends who always seems to find time to help out our family. She has booked us a room at the Comfort Suites, a new motel in Marion. The brochure says it has a pool which turns out to be too warm and small to swim in, but not quite warm enough to be a hot tub. I lie on my back and float, then run in place, and float again. They have freshly baked chocolate chip cookies at the desk which makes up for not having a pool.

Betty and two other friends of Mom's, Anne Ganz, and Irma Maidenberg are taking us to dinner at the Country Club. Bill and his 17-year-old son, Josh will arrive on a later plane and drive from Indianapolis. Josh has told Bill that he wants to go to the funeral. He doesn't know why, it's something he just needs to do, so Bill is coming too. I leave a note for them in case they want to join us. Dusty and his son Jacob plan to spend the night in Indianapolis with Dorothy and come with her the next day.

Betty tells me to look around the country club to see how it has changed. What she doesn't know, and what I don't tell her now, is that I refused to come here with my parents. When I was in high school, Mom and Dad were invited to submit a membership to the Marion Country Club. We were the first Jewish family ever asked to join. Of course, there were no blacks, Hispanics, Indians or anyone who wasn't white and Christian. It was to be large step forward for the community to enroll a Jewish family.

116

After their membership was submitted, we began receiving phone calls which ranged from hateful to actually threatening. My parents did not receive enough votes to become members. I was in high school at the time. A few years later my parents were invited again and became members along with several other Jewish families. I never wanted to join a club with a group of people who hated me like that.

The room is quiet and the food is excellent. Even though it is the day before my father's funeral, the conversation centers around my mother and they begin telling Charlotte stories. Anne says to me: "People in this town still miss your mother and not a day goes by that we don't speak of her fondly. You knew where you stood with Charlotte."

"That's right," I add, "in the brain and out the mouth. Sometimes I didn't want to know where I stood with my mother."

Anne, Betty, and Irma laugh. "Well, I liked that about her," says Irma.

"That's right," says Betty, "no second guessing Charlotte. How are you dealing with your dad's death? I know you had a hard time after your mom died."

"It was different with Mom. She died so young, when Myrrhia was only two and they were much alike. I wish that they had more time together. I could talk with

Mom about feelings; I just felt closer to her. I loved my dad, but it's different." We share more stories about my mother and laugh. It's fun to talk about her without the wrenching grief that bit at the heels of my life for so many years after she died.

The next morning I encounter Bill in the lobby of the motel. I have just returned from a run along the river. It was much quieter than that white water rush that was here in May when Dusty and I came to get Dad.

I say hi. Bill seems nervous. I tell him that the desk wouldn't give me his room number.

"Why?"

"Maybe they're afraid I'll assassinate you. We're in room 217."

"Where's Dusty?"

"He's coming in with Dorothy and Betty Fleck's daughter, Debbie. We're all going to meet at the temple and then go to the grave site. After the funeral we'll return to the temple for lunch. People are dropping off food there." Jewish custom seems to require a meal with everything except for Yom Kippur. On Yom Kippur you commit the ultimate sacrifice for God and fast for a day. I rarely have made it through a whole day of fasting, but I have trouble eating after funerals.

The day is another version of Midwest gray. The sky is low and seems to hover directly above our heads and the air has a fall chill. Wearing the knit cap Myrrhia made for me is a good idea. A tent has been erected over the grave site. It says on it: "Estates of Serenity". I whisper to Billy: "This isn't a serene state anymore, not with Mom and Dad here."

Tony, my childhood friend, leads the service. He does an excellent job. Bill doesn't say much. I read my little poem. Dusty tries to talk about how Dad found peace and starts to choke up. A woman speaks up who I don't know. She says: "That's how he was when he was dying, but let's remember him how he was here, powerful and vital. He told us all about Nature Conservancy, fought for his beliefs, you could count on him."

"That's right," one of the women who worked for Dad at his store says. "If you had a problem, he would help you. He called my doctor in Indianapolis when he thought the doctor wasn't attending to my leg."

"He helped my husband," says another.

I begin to sob and lean into Josh's shoulder.

Another woman who I don't know adds. "Bill always had strong beliefs and opinions. After temple services he would tell me that I should write letters about issues and he tried to tell me what to put into those letters. I told him that if I wrote letters, they would express my beliefs and he might not like them."

"He loved his children," says someone else. "He always told me the story about how his son sold his daughter for a quarter." I nudge Bill and whisper, "You'd still like to sell me off."

Irma says: "Bill and Charlotte must have done something right. Look at these three children here. They would make any parent proud." I look at my brothers. Billy looks handsome in his suit, and Dusty is wearing a sweater which accents the green of his eyes. It's nice to see him without his uniform of shorts and a t-shirt.

Before leaving the cemetery, I take a minute to look at the gravestones, for what may be the last time ever. Dad lies in between two powerful women, his mom and his wife. He will certainly be well cared for here. The gray tombstones stand in dark relief against the lighter gray of the sky. I feel like I'm in a black and white movie. I only need a black chauffeured limousine to drive me away from the cemetery. Instead I push some of her boys' toys aside and climb into Debbie Fleck's green suburban.

At the temple, I'm ushered toward the food line. Betty says, "People are hungry and they can't eat until you eat. Mourners must eat first. Here are the traditional hard boiled eggs. But there are also deviled eggs and I think they count as hardboiled eggs." I decide on the deviled eggs.

People come up to talk. They tell me they're sorry about my dad and then begin to tell me more stories about my mother and how much they miss her. It must have been hard for Dorothy to be Dad's second wife in this town.

Afterwards my brothers and I take our families for a walk down by the river. Mark Russell comes along, Dusty's best friend from childhood. Myrrhia and Jacob have been close since they were babies. They are forcefully sharing their opinions, hitting each other and laughing. It feels familiar and good.

Bill says his back hurts and slows his pace. I seize this opportunity to be alone with him and also slow down. My hands are shaking but I ask anyway. "Why did you stop talking to me?"

He stops walking and so do I. He looks at me, then looks at the trees and says: "That's over. To talk about it would bring it all up again." He takes off his glasses, looks me in the eyes and says emphatically, "Dad is dead and let's go on."

I wish he were willing to share his feelings and hear mine. Maybe now isn't the best time, maybe there never will be a time. I love Billy. Wondering if he sees the sadness in my eyes, I reply, "all right."

That night Mom's friends want to take us to dinner again. They suggest the country club or Erma's steak house. I choose Erma's. For one, it's not the country club and it's more relaxed. Bill suggests that we treat for the meal and I appreciate his thoughtfulness.

In sixth grade the teacher went around the room asking us what we intended "to be" when we grew up. Tony at eleven-years-old said he wanted to be mayor of Marion. I forget what the rest of us said, but we all grew up and moved away and became doctors and psychologists and teachers, but Tony stayed in Marion and ran for mayor. Marion's Ku Klux Klan did not take the idea of a Jewish mayor lightly and burned a cross on his front yard. He adds: "After that, they gerrymandered the district so no Democrat ever has a chance of being elected to the state legislature from here."

Myrrhia is shocked. She turns to me and says: "Why haven't you told me these things about the country club, the lynching and about the Flu Klux Klan? I'm at school taking classes on racism and gender and you don't even tell me this happened to you."

"I don't know, Myrrhia. I guess it's partly because I don't like to think about it." "Well I want to hear about it."

"Okay, some other time you and I can talk about this."

My mind starts a verse of the song: "Back home again in Indiana," where I no longer be.

Jenny, Tony's wife is staring at Josh, Jacob, and Myrrhia. They all have on huge baggy pants. Myrrhia has a ring in her eyebrow and Jacob's hair is bleached blonde. She turns to me: "My kids don't look like that. Is that what is going to happen to them?"

I reassure her. "Probably not if they stay in the Midwest."

We are putting on our coats and saying goodbyes. Irma Maidenberg pulls me aside. "Do you really know who your father was?"

Why is she asking me this now? I think I knew my father both sane and demented, both in charge and helpless. This is not territory I want to enter, especially not here and now. I look her straight in the eyes and say: "I know my dad. All of my dad, believe me, I know him."

Later that night, though, I think about her question. What could she have meant? That Dad wasn't my father? Maybe my mother had an affair. It would be exciting to find out I have another father. I have visions of telling my friends about this, maybe going into therapy. I realize that I'm enjoying being the character in my own soap opera. You would think that I've had enough drama with Dad's shenanigans. I remind myself that these stories all seem more interesting from a distance. I find it difficult to believe that I have another father, but I decide to call her tomorrow morning. I want to know what she means.

Irma is home, but with a sore throat. I ask her if she can talk and she says sure.

"Do you remember your comment last night, about not really knowing who my father is?"

"Did I say that?"

"Yes, you said as I was leaving, that I didn't really know my father."

"Oh, Helen Rae, that was just one of those comments. Like you really don't know your father, now do you? He had a whole life before you were even born. We only know some of our parents."

"Is that it?"

Irma laughs. "I really didn't mean anything. It's just that."

I put down the phone startled again to find myself a little disappointed that the story didn't develop more. But for Dad not to be my father, Mom would have been a different person. That sounds farfetched and when I think about what this all really would mean, I must admit that I'm relieved not be plagued with uncertainty about my parentage. I think Dad has provided enough drama for awhile.

The next day Bill leaves early for Indianapolis to catch his plane. Dusty and I want to go to Asherwood and hike before I leave from Fort Wayne later that afternoon.

At breakfast, with Dusty watching, I give Bill the contents of the safety box which I have been managing as conservator. I am no longer responsible for Dad's ashes or the financial records I carried on the plane from Santa Cruz. I feel much lighter.

On the way to Asherwood I realize that we are only two miles from the Frances Slocum trail, my favorite place to spend time with Dad. On Sundays, if he didn't have too much work at the store, he would ask each of

120

us what we wanted to do. When the weather was nice I always chose to hike the Frances Slocum Trail. It was named after a woman, who was kidnapped by the Mississinewa Indians when she was a little girl. After her parents died her brothers decided to find her. Several of the Indians told them about a woman who they thought might have some white blood. They went to visit the tribe to speak to her. They were directed to a squaw sitting next to her pot outside her teepee. The brothers introduced themselves, but they did not believe this dark skinned Indian was their sister. After the squaw had decided that they were good men, she lifted up her skirt and showed them that where her skin had been protected by the sun, it was still white. They wanted her to return with them, but she had a husband, children and a life with the Indians and chose to stay. When we hiked the portion of the trail the Indians transversed when they kidnapped her, I always wondered if I would return with my brothers or choose to remain in this forest I loved so deeply. I had never realized before how close Asherwood was to Francis Slocum State Park and this was the first time I had walked these woods this time of year with snow on the ground.

Since she was a little girl, David and I have been taking Myrrhia on backpacking trips into the Sierras but have never hiked with her in the Midwest.

Myrrhia walks next to me, while Dusty and David are behind us talking. Myrrhia and I decide that if we hold hands it will help keep them warm against the winter chill. The terrain in Indiana is different in that the countryside is heavily wooded and flat. There are no breath taking vistas of rocks, nor fast rushing mountain streams. Dusty guides us to a small ice covered pond where once in a while a rabbit darts across the trail.

A sanctuary for birds has been built. It is in honor of Mrs. Gottschalk. Once, she took me bird watching. We had to be still and look at birds through binoculars. She could identify subtle variations in colors of their breasts and the way the feathers lined up on their wings. I found it interesting for about five minutes and then began directing my attention to the variety of bugs crawling on the ground. At the sanctuary are two owls, an eagle, and a turkey vulture, all birds of prey who kill the birds Mrs. Gottschalk enjoyed watching. Myrrhia is upset that they might be holding birds captive, but David points out that they have been either permanently injured or are rehabilitating. Still, we don't like to see the birds in a pen and decide to leave.

We have time before our plane departs and visit a used book store. Dusty finds books about the Frances Slocum trail and reads me various versions of the story. We hug him goodby and take off to the Fort Wayne airport. I think this is the last time I will ever see my home town. As the plane rises in the air above the clouds, sunshine streams in through the windows. The light is blinding but the warmth feels cuddly and soft.

121

PART 15
Santa Cruz

It's the beginning of March and Liat and I climb the last hill and emerge from the redwood forest. She runs across the golf course and slowly lowers her red furry body into the pond. Only her head is visible, as she disappears into the water. She soaks, dumps her black nose in and then throws the water up over her head and emerges from the pond coughing and shaking her coat. This is Liat's first dip of the year. The sun is shining and I enjoy its warmth in contrast to the damp coolness of the forest.

As I begin to run across the golf course, I take time to experience the pleasure of each foot landing and pushing off from the soft grass. I carefully make my way down the steep hill which leads to the trail back home. The cyglosseums are beginning to bloom and their blue lace makes a nice contrast with the delicate white and green of the narcissus lining the trail. After Dad came to Santa Cruz, I sought the solitude of these paths. Often I felt an emptiness deep in the belly followed by a flood of longing. Then I walked, allowing myself time to mourn the father I was losing.

About ten years ago I asked him how he felt about aging and death. He told me not to worry, that he wouldn't die. He cited as an example falling off a bicycle and recovering without a scratch. Instead of convincing me that he was invincible, I was impressed with how well his denial worked. And then, somehow he had the awareness that he was dying, he didn't know what was killing him, but he had visited the emergency room in Marion only a year and a half before the cancer appeared in his back. And about a month before he was taken to the hospital in Petaluma, he called to tell me he wanted to be buried in my garden. Did he have a prescient knowing or were there somatic signals that his brain deciphered, Alzheimers and all? We all will die and are rarely able to choose the specifics of the end. My mom and David's father had cancer and died with self awareness and dignity. Alzheimers rendered Dad a fool but that was only part of the time. His humor, passion, will and love of life shone through despite the tangled plaques in his brain.

Dad loved life and now every time I run, I try to be aware and to enjoy the green canopy of leaves over head, the way the smells and breezes change with each bend and turn, and to be grateful that my body still can move this way, can still run and bring me such pleasure. This morning I notice that this is the first time since Dad came to Santa Cruz that I am running this trail without sad memories and longings for my father. It must be spring.

About the Author

Helen Resneck-Sannes is a psychologist in private practice in Santa Cruz California. She also teaches and lectures nationally and internationally for the International Institute for Bioenergetic Analysis.

While know for her publications in psychology journals and books, she has also published short stories and poems. A chapter from Father's Rooms is already available in an anthology of stories about Alzheimer's called Love is Ageless. Writing the memoir was healing not only for herself, but her family as well. She hopes it can help other who are trying to come to terms with this disease in themselves and the people they love.

Printed in the United States
936100005B